INVISIBLE BLACKNESS

A LOUISIANA FAMILY IN THE AGE OF RACIAL PASSING

KATY MORLAS SHANNON

Louisiana State University Press   Baton Rouge

Published with the assistance of the V. Ray Cardozier Fund

Published by Louisiana State University Press
lsupress.org

Copyright © 2025 by Katy Morlas Shannon
All rights reserved. Except in the case of brief quotations used in articles or reviews, no part of this publication may be produced or transmitted in any format or by any means without written permission of Louisiana State University Press.

Manufactured in the United States of America
First printing

DESIGNER: Michelle A. Neustrom
TYPEFACES: Minion Pro, text; Gotham, display
PRINTER AND BINDER: Sheridan Books, Inc.

JACKET IMAGE: Detail of a carte de visite featuring Rosina "Rosa" Downs, a formerly enslaved child from New Orleans, ca. 1864. Photograph by Charles Paxson. Gladstone Collection of African American Photographs, Prints and Photographs Division of the Library of Congress.

Cataloging-in-publication data are available at the Library of Congress.

ISBN 978-0-8071-8382-3 (cloth) | ISBN 978-0-8071-8457-8 (epub) | ISBN 978-0-8071-8458-5 (pdf)

for my beloved husband
Robin Shannon
and in memory of
Marguerite Tregre Grossinger
and
Major Francis Ernest Dumas

Stranger, misunderstood by your own country,
You always knew how to love it!
—V. E. Rillieux, "Une Larme, à Aristide Mary," 1893

Caste makes distinctions where God has made none.
—Charles Sumner, U.S. senator

CONTENTS

Author's Note xi

Introduction: Creoles and Free People of Color in Early Louisiana 1

Prologue 22

1 The Issue of Her Body: Alice Thomasson 29
2 Being Once Free: Alice Thomasson 38
3 All the Social Qualities of a Gentleman: Alice Thomasson Grice 47
4 A Complexion like Alabaster: Marguerite Tregre 60
5 St. Margaret, Keeper of Furnished Rooms: Marguerite Tregre Grossinger 73
6 Tears in the Telling: Georgina Lombard Gaal 83
7 Scratch the Surface: Marie Heno Forstall 98
8 An Upright, Honorable Existence: Marguerite Tregre Grossinger and the Grice Children 113
9 A Menace to the Purity of the White Race: Marie Heno Forstall 125
10 Tearing Down the Bars: Marie Heno Forstall 138

Epilogue 152

Acknowledgments 157

Notes 161

Index 181

AUTHOR'S NOTE

I would like to briefly discuss the usage of some terms in *Invisible Blackness*. I do not use the phrase "African American" because the people profiled here, as well as many of their descendants, would never have identified as such. They considered themselves Creole, not American. I use the word "enslaved" in place of "slave," but the word "slave" appears because it was the legal term used on all recorded documents at the time. "Free people of color," "free person of color," "free woman of color," and "free man of color" were all legal terms recognized by the state and were used by individuals within that community to refer to themselves. Today we recognize the words "mulatto," "quadroon," and "octoroon" as divisive and inappropriate, but for the families I write about, these terms were very real, very much a part of their everyday lives, and they had a significant impact on their life experiences. In fact, these racial designations were legal terms and ultimately led to a landmark Louisiana Supreme Court ruling that would negatively affect countless individuals. I also frequently use the terms "people of color" or "Creoles of color," because many of the individuals included in this work would not necessarily have identified as "Black."

In historian Amrita Chakrabarti Myers's study of free people of color in Charleston, she noted, "With regards to identifying free persons in terms of color, I make it a point to refer to individuals as 'black,' 'brown,' 'person of color,' 'negro,' 'mulatto' . . . according to how they are identified in archival documents." Myers drew on the language of primary sources. This is the approach I take in this work to both enslaved individuals and free people of color. Phenotypes and descriptors designating fractional African ancestry were recognized by the church, the state, and Louisiana natives of all racial backgrounds.[1]

I also reached out to present-day Creoles in New Orleans who are actively engaged in the local community. I asked them to review my use of language. I also requested that they tell me how they choose to identify and how their ancestors identified. I would never wish to write about people using language that they would not have used to refer to themselves or chosen to identify with. I tried my best to stay true to how they would have chosen to describe themselves and to approach this topic with sensitivity while remaining historically accurate.

INVISIBLE
BLACKNESS

INTRODUCTION

Creoles and Free People of Color in Early Louisiana

I cannot remember a time when I wasn't keenly aware that most of us in south Louisiana—at least the ones whose families have been present for generations—are all interconnected. Yet I don't believe that was ever explained to me. It is a mystery how I intuited that interwoven family networks, bridging seemingly insurmountable racial divides, were characteristic of my home and my ancestors. Perhaps my sincere devotion to my Catholic faith, which taught me that we are all brothers and sisters in Christ, was responsible. Maybe it was the fact that my parents had never instilled in me the "us-versus-them" mentality with which they were raised. It's likely that the many people of various shades and backgrounds I observed growing up in the New Orleans metropolitan area contributed as well. I was a child who watched and listened and was obsessed with details; I do the same now. My observant, precocious nature and propensity for eavesdropping seem the most likely source. Thus, I was shocked when, as an adolescent, I learned that interconnections across the color line were unknown to many people and were purposely unrecognized by many others.

I set out on a quest to discover the intricacies of my own family tree, certain it would inform my understanding of the biological and cultural bonds that inextricably link Louisiana Creoles of all races and backgrounds. I could then share this, show people actual data in black letters on white papers found in courthouses, archives, churches, and vital records across the state, data that could not be denied. I could not have articulated this calling in any meaningful way when it first gripped me. I just knew I had an insatiable curiosity and that my questions had never received satisfactory answers. So, I began asking more questions and journeying through Louisiana's past by car, computer, and archive.

The newfound freedom I received when I was given a car my sophomore year at Louisiana State University provided me with the means to start my search. I began by exiting off the interstate into a swamp. It was like going back in time. I found myself immediately engulfed in cypress trees and palmettos before emerging into a vast sea of sugarcane. I had arrived in St. James and St. John the Baptist Parishes, where my maternal grandmother's roots were deep. I had grown up hearing my great-grandparents tell stories of their youth spent on the edge of these cane fields. I drove countless hours along the River Road, mostly by myself, touring historic homes, stopping at cemeteries, and exploring abandoned plantations. I learned the most common family names of the area because I saw them in the cemeteries and never forgot them. I became familiar with the places and landmarks that characterized these parishes because I stood there and observed them. Before I entered any archive, I was living history.

At the same time as I was traveling Louisiana's back roads in search of my family's history, I was reminded of it every time I returned to campus. I was living in LSU's East Campus apartments in a unit made to accommodate four people. One of my roommates was a light-skinned African American young woman. Her last name was Guillory. It had been my great-grandmother's maiden name. I immediately suspected that we shared common ancestors.

Compelled to know more, I braved the commanding edifice that was Hill Memorial Library and walked into my first archive. Intimidated by the marble halls and wood paneling, I felt like a child sneaking into an adult party. I worried that I needed permission to be there. Yet everyone there, from the student workers to the archivists, was gracious and welcoming. I had recently read about historian Gwendolyn Midlo Hall's slavery database and wanted to see it for myself. At that time, it was available only on CD-ROM. The archivist informed me that I was the first person to ask to use it. She located the item, called the main library, and sent me just across campus, passing crepe myrtles and live oaks, to work on a computer in the basement of Middleton Library. I input my family names into the database. It proved what I already knew. We were not a plantation dynasty the likes of the families of Oak Alley or Houmas House, but from the earliest days of colonial Louisiana, my ancestors had enslaved other human beings. That meant I was walking among the descendants of individuals formerly enslaved by my family. I was certain this was true for most people in Louisiana. How could we continue to ignore this? So many things remained unsaid. How could there be healing, growth, or change when the ties that bound us were denied and the oppression, prejudices, and violence of the not-so-distant past went unacknowledged?

I soon realized there could be no discussion about slavery without including both the enslaved and those enslaving them, Black and white, slave and free. Most significantly, professors, curators, teachers, and your average person walking down the street needed to know that these groups were not static or mutually exclusive. Enslaved people, slaveholders, free people of color, European craftsmen, overseers, steamboat captains, and merchants—members of all these groups were interrelated, biologically connected, in some cases acknowledged as family, and in others denied. The brutality of the chattel system invariably meant that the haunting image of a slaveholder inflicting violence on an enslaved person, a defining element of the American historical narrative, frequently went much deeper. The people who callously sold enslaved people without a second thought, the men who held the whip, and the women whose slaps reverberated through the dining room were often the fathers, grandparents, aunts and uncles, and siblings of the enslaved people they abused, manipulated, and traumatized both psychologically and physically.

My sixth-great-grandfather, Joseph Gregoire Guillory, had children with a woman named Margarita (sometimes Marguerite), who in the eyes of the law was his property. Guillory promised to free Margarita and their children and went so far as to have a local schoolteacher draft written proof of his decision. However, the man he chose to free them was not recognized by law to oversee manumission. When Guillory's wife died and her succession was settled, Guillory's white children inherited their enslaved half-siblings. Guillory then pulled a knife on his son and forcibly abducted Margarita and her children from his son's household in an effort to give them their freedom that he had promised. Thus began a protracted legal battle in which Guillory's legitimate children fought to hold their half-siblings in slavery. Ultimately Margarita and her children would be freed. More than two centuries later, descendants of Guillory's white children and of his formerly enslaved children would live together while attending Louisiana State University. If this was my reality, it could also be true for so many other families.

These relationships were not always characterized by violence and betrayal. In fact, some existed as loving families. My research, and that of other scholars and genealogists, would uncover numerous examples of interracial couples and their children who lived in every way as husband and wife, parents and children, except in the eyes of the law. The families profiled in this work are examples.

After receiving my master's degree in history, I began my career as a professional historian, focusing on enslaved communities along the River Road between New Orleans and Baton Rouge. While researching benevolent societies and medical practices in St. John the Baptist Parish, I learned about Dr. Blaise Duhé, a Creole of color who provided medical care on the east bank of the parish in the early twentieth century. Soon after, I met Alan Duhé in a Facebook group. He was engaged in genealogical research to trace his enslaved ancestors. We discovered that we are, in fact, distant cousins. Messaging with him inspired me to investigate our shared Duhé ancestors and the world they inhabited.

Marie Baselite Cambre was just a young woman when she became a widow. Her husband Jacques Duhé left her with an infant son who bore his name and with a small home on a piece of land on the east bank of the Mississippi River in St. John the Baptist Parish where sugarcane was cultivated on a small scale. The land was the property of the widow of Eli Duhé, née Marianne Pontiff, Jacques' mother. With the death of Jacques, something would have to be done about the property.[1]

The Duhés were Creoles. Yet so were most of the people they enslaved. The word *Creole* hearkens back to its origins as the Portugese *criollo*, meaning "born in the colony." Creoles were individuals who were born not in Europe or Africa like their ancestors but in Louisiana. The word transcended race. In some of the earliest documents, enslaved people were described as Creole. Creoles shared a cultural heritage: they spoke French, practiced Catholicism, embraced the civil code rather than common law, and harbored views more aligned with France, Spain, and the Caribbean than with their birthplace. Unlike their Anglo counterparts, Creole women had property rights and inherited their share on the deaths of their parents and husbands.

Baselite needed a means to provide for her young son. A succession was filed in which she represented her child's interests, and an inventory of Eli Duhé's property was made. There were cows and pigs to provide the family with sustenance, horses and mules to work the land, and sixteen enslaved people to relieve the Duhé family of the most backbreaking labor. Henri, a fifty-year-old man from the Congo; Fanny, a forty-year-old woman also from the Congo; and Jean Louis and Celestin, Creoles in their thirties, planted, plowed, and harvested the fields, likely alongside the Duhé sons. This was not a large plantation, and enslaver and enslaved would have worked together to bring in the crops. It was like a little village, a complex of buildings housing multiple generations of a family both free and enslaved.

Jacques and Baselite had lived in a modest Creole cottage made of timber frame and bousillage, a mixture of clay and moss used as infill that was similar to wattle and daub. Such cottages had two main rooms, typically a parlor and a bedroom, and two smaller cabinet rooms used for storage; some had stairs to an upstairs attic space, where additional bedrooms might be located. The house was surrounded by galleries—what Americans might call porches—in front and back, functioning at times as outdoor living space. This was a uniquely Creole construction, combining the building techniques of Europeans, Africans, and Native Americans to create an architectural style best suited to the conditions and climate of south Louisiana. An outdoor kitchen would have serviced both the Duhés and the enslaved laborers. It was the domain of Françoise, a forty-five-year-old Creole mother of four who was responsible for the cooking and laundering. Her youngest children, Adam and Joseph, were eight and six years old, respectively.

Though Baselite, her mother-in-law, and sisters-in-laws would certainly have had household chores and tasks to complete, they were spared the hardest labor. Modeste, Françoise's eldest daughter, did the housework, while her other daughter Julienne watched over and cared for the children. The sisters were seventeen and fourteen, respectively. Twenty-year-old Eve, a Creole, also labored in the house. Marie Louise, an elderly Creole woman, and two orphaned siblings—Marguerite, age four, and Pierre, age two—likely helped with small tasks. Meanwhile the presence of Eve's children proved that the Duhé family likely contained members of all races. Every enslaved man, woman, and child on the plantation was described as "negro," except for Eve's daughters—five-year-old Zeline and three-year-old Rosalie—who appeared in the inventory of the Duhé's property as "mulatresses." Eve's youngest child, Seraphin, only eighteen months old, was described as a "negro," though it is possible that he was also of mixed racial ancestry. These designations were by no means an exact science.

A few years later, when she was around twenty-five, Baselite remarried. Her new husband, Joseph Vicknair, lived longer than her first one had. She had several children with him before his death from tuberculosis in 1850.[2] Baselite raised her six children and took over the management of Vicknair's humble plantation. Despite the small scale of her enterprise, she referred to herself as a "planter" to census takers.[3] By 1860, her eldest son, Jacques Duhé, was married with a child and working as the overseer on the plantation.[4] At the same time, on Mt. Airy Plantation just a few miles upriver from his mother's, Jacques Duhé met a mixed-race enslaved domestic laborer named Edwige Duplantier. When she was born, Edwige was considered the property of Armand Duplantier, his wife, his mother-in-law, and his brothers-in-law, the Fortins. On the dissolution of the partnership between Duplantier and the Fortins, Edwige was listed in "Lot 2" of the assets of the business. The Fortins received "Lot 2"—Edwige and her family—in the division of the property. Shortly thereafter they sold the plantation and the enslaved people on it, including Edwige and her children, to Joseph LeBourgeois. Edwige's experience illustrates that even though she was the child of her enslaver, she did not receive any acknowledgment of that relationship or any benefits because of it. Yet she would always identify herself as Edwige Duplantier, taking back her agency after emancipation and revealing the truth of her parentage. Over the course of a decade spanning both slavery and emancipation, Edwige gave birth to four children with Jacques Duhé: Emile in 1860, Edmond in 1863, Celina in 1868, and Edward in 1870. These children took his surname, they candidly identified their father in marriage records, and their descendants acknowledged him in their death records. Jacques Duhé lived with his wife and white children in a house not far from Edwige and his children, who by law were deemed "colored." In a small, isolated community, he maintained two separate families, one white and one of color.[5]

These were not the only Duhés of Afro-Creole descent. Evariste Duhé, born into slavery on the Vicknair plantation, was the son of an enslaved woman and Zephirin Duhé, Baselite's brother-in-law and Jacques' uncle. When Evariste enlisted in the Union Army to fight for freedom during the Civil War, the American enrolling officer, unable to understand French and unfamiliar with Creole names, assigned him the name John Cupel.[6] On gaining his freedom, Evariste worked and saved for his children. His son Dr. Blaise Duhé obtained a bachelor's degree from Fisk University and then attended medical school at Iowa University.[7] He returned to St. John the Baptist Parish to practice medicine there. Another of his sons, Lawrence Duhé, took up the clarinet and became a well-known jazz musician. He played with Kid Ory, who grew up on a neighboring plantation, and King Oliver, eventually relocating to Chicago.[8]

Jacques Duhé was the great-grandfather of my great-grandmother, Bertha Duhé Bourgeois. I knew my Granny well. Growing up, I saw her almost every weekend. She lived until I was fifteen years old. I knew her father was Gaston Duhé. What I didn't realize until adulthood was that her father grew up in the same community with another Gaston Duhé, only seven years his senior. One Gaston Duhé—my great-great-grandfather—was considered white; the other Gaston Duhé was labeled Black. My ancestor could vote, send his children to good schools, sit where he wanted to on public transportation, and stand trial before a jury of his peers. The other Gaston Duhé, who was considered Black, could not. They shared a common ancestry, language, religion, and place of birth; yet their lives could not be more different because the white supremacy of Louisiana—in fact, of the South and of the entire country—demanded that they adhere to a rigid hierarchy that made it abundantly clear that some lives were worth more than others, even in the supposed land of the free. New Orleans judge Hugh C. Cage candidly and succinctly summed up the situation in 1924: "Race prejudice in Louisiana is as concrete a fact as caste is in India. . . . This is a condition not a theory."[9]

In her groundbreaking work on caste in America, Isabel Wilkerson described what separated these Gaston Duhés, and so many others like him, as a caste system that provided the "infrastructure of our divisions," creating a "human hierarchy, the subconscious code of instructions for maintain[ing], in our case, a four-hundred-year-old social order." Though a social construct, this system had profoundly real consequences. It declared one set of human beings superior to another, ranking them according to "ancestry and often immutable traits, traits that would be neutral in the abstract but are ascribed life-and-death meaning in a hierarchy favoring the dominant caste whose forbears designed it . . . [using] rigid, often arbitrary boundaries to keep the ranked groupings apart, distinct from one another and in their assigned places." Here in the United States this "structure of human hierarchy" is based on race. Some scholars take issue with Wilkerson's assertion that a racial caste system exists, contending that the argument she deploys discounts certain significant nuances. Wilkerson's model is not perfect. However, when examining the tripartite racial order that existed in Louisiana in the eighteenth and nineteenth centuries and its socioeconomic aspects, her discussion of race as a caste system offers important insights and is often very accurate. The fact that a judge in Louisiana compared the racial hierarchy that existed to a caste system underscores this.[10]

In many ways race is a uniquely American phenomenon, or at least it was at first. Before their arrival in the Americas, African people did not see themselves as Black but as tribal groups. They were Mandinga, Congo, Bambara—each with its own distinct cultures, languages, and histories. They did not see themselves as united in their Blackness, just as newly arrived immigrants from Europe were not white: they were English, French, Spanish, Irish, and German. When, however, the United States chose to embrace race-based chattel slavery as a viable labor system, concepts like whiteness and Blackness emerged. Wilkerson compared the racial caste system of the United States to that of India and Nazi Germany: "Each version relied on stigmatizing those deemed inferior to justify the dehumanization necessary to keep the lowest-ranked people at the bottom to rationalize the protocols of enforcement." Slavery and later the Jim Crow South could not have existed without this necessary dehumanization and the passing down of this racial hierarchy over generations.[11]

This book explores those boundaries and assigned places and the courageous men and women who chose to challenge them. Sadly, this hierarchy is based on the principle that proximity to whiteness is what determines the rung on which a person stands in the racial caste system. People of mixed race, for a time, received more benefits for being closer to what society deemed "white." Yet as the U.S. racial order constricted, their rights were stripped away. "Caste is fixed and rigid," Wilkerson noted. "Race is fluid and superficial, subject to periodic redefinition to meet the needs of the dominant caste in what is now the United States." This "ladder of humanity" determined access to power and resources.[12]

Just like the rest of the United States, Louisiana existed under a racial caste system. Yet it was not the dualistic Black and white caste system that existed in the rest of the country. Instead, Creole Louisiana operated within a tripartite caste system, consisting of whites, free people of color, and the enslaved population. In fact, for most of Louisiana's history, there were additional categories based on varying skin color, which in turn depended on the amount of African ancestry one possessed. Racial descriptors such as mulatto, quadroon, and octoroon were regularly used to convey the fractional sum of African ancestry present in an individual: one-half for a mulatto, one-quarter for a quadroon, and one-eighth for an octoroon. We might balk at the use of these terms today, but in a caste system based on the way a person looked, obsessions with phenotype not only made sense but also significantly shaped society. These designations factored into the autonomy an individual possessed, as well as how the world perceived her, because proximity to whiteness influenced power and resources. In exceptional circumstances, this proximity could even allow for a shift to the dominant caste.

Why does Louisiana so often prove exceptional in U.S. history? What can we learn about the American caste system in all its incarnations, both then and now, by studying Louisiana? And how did a Black man named Gaston Duhé and a white man named Gaston Duhé come of age together in the same tight-knit community, surrounded by people who had known their families for generations and were aware of their ancestral and cultural connections? We must look back to the earliest days of Louisiana to fully understand.

Louisiana became the first permanent European settlement in the Mississippi Valley under French rule. At the time, approximately seventy thousand Native Americans from various tribes called the region home. By 1702, 140 French settlers were living in the area that is today Mobile, Alabama. They were expected to engage in trade with the Choctaw and Chickasaw tribes and serve as a buffer to British expansion.[13]

Constantly at war and in need of funds, the French crown ignored the new colony and the needs of its first settlers. Severe supply shortages led to the threat of starvation and the need to rely primarily on enslaved labor and the assistance of Native Americans. French settlers and Native Americans became strongly interconnected, creating a frontier exchange economy in which Indigenous people and Europeans traded furs and subsistence crops, with no real commercial market outside the colony. The population consisted of *coureurs de bois* (French backwoodsmen), soldiers, craftsmen, Native Americans, and missionary priests, all of whom had little to no interaction with France and were left to survive on their own.[14]

Eventually France handed control of the colony over to the Company of the West. Led by John Law, the company promised to reduce the crown's debt and turn Louisiana into a thriving colony and source of funds for France. Although Law's efforts ultimately failed and the "Mississippi Bubble" burst, his actions brought about significant changes in the new colony that would have a lasting impact. Louisiana's capital was moved to New Orleans in 1718. The population grew as wealthy Frenchmen arrived to claim concessions of land along the Mississippi River. German peasants, lured with false promises of a land likened to the Garden of Eden, settled just upriver from New Orleans. They had been brought in to engage in agricultural labor. Law used whatever means he could to increase the colony's population, forcibly bringing in impressed criminals and women from hospitals and asylums across France.[15] Louisiana, already considered a wild, savage land, was now the home of the criminals and rejects of France. Although the population had increased to about five thousand in 1721, the colony dwindled to only two thousand inhabitants by the end of the decade. Disease, famine, exposure to the elements, and the challenges of establishing a colony in the middle of an isolated swamp led to high death rates and caused many people to do whatever they could to return to Europe.[16]

A significant influence on Louisiana's population arrived in 1719 with the forced migration of approximately six thousand enslaved Africans. The majority came from the Senegambian region of West Africa and were highly skilled. They were adept in agricultural pursuits and brought with them knowledge of the cultivation of rice, corn, tobacco, and indigo. They excelled in technologies and craftsmanship that would prove essential to the success of the colony. Enslaved Africans and Native Americans interacted regularly and formed intimate relationships that prevented the French from dominating. Even though the Code Noir was implemented in 1724 to regulate the lives of the enslaved and exert some control by European settlers, slaves found that frontier conditions enabled them to challenge French authority. With the aid of Native Americans, enslaved Africans formed runaway communities in the cypress swamps, planned revolts, and maintained an autonomy that would have been impossible in a more stable, controlled colonial environment.[17]

Because Africans made up most of the colony's population, they were able to maintain a degree of power despite their enslaved condition. The French recognized their dependence on the enslaved population and frequently engaged in more relaxed, fluid relationships with enslaved Africans than those that existed in other colonies. Only one slave ship arrived after 1736, limiting the population of enslaved Africans in the colony to those already present and those born there through natural increase. As a result, a strong Afro-Creole culture developed.[18]

On November 28, 1729, warriors of the Natchez tribe killed more than two hundred French settlers and captured over three hundred enslaved people and fifty French women and children. Ten percent of the colony's white population died in the attack. As a result of the Natchez Revolt, an already stagnant economy experienced a harsh downturn. The next decade in Louisiana was characterized by military and economic failures. The French launched retaliatory military campaigns against the Natchez and Chickasaw tribes.[19] Despite efforts to engage in the tobacco trade, the colony experienced inflation, poor agricultural conditions, and a devastating hurricane. No new immigrants arrived, and apart from one vessel carrying enslaved Africans after 1736, no more enslaved Africans were forcibly brought to French Louisiana.

Life in the French colony was characterized by isolation, struggle, chaos, and the coming together of diverse ethnic groups to survive. After suffering a devastating loss in the Seven Years' War, also known as the French and Indian War, France decided to unburden itself of the failing colony. In 1762, Louisiana was given to Spain, France's ally against England's New World expansion.

French colonial Louisiana was a wild frontier that had never experienced stable population growth. In contrast, Spain's four-decade rule over Louisiana brought prosperity, stability, and dramatic expansion. However, colonists were skeptical of Spanish rule, and the newly arrived Spanish governor met with resistance that would ultimately lead to a revolt. A second generation of French and German settlers born in the colony, many of them planters or merchants, grew to hold prominence in Louisiana. Known as Creoles, this ruling class opposed the strict trade regulations implemented by Spain and fought to maintain local autonomy. It is important to note that enslaved people born in Louisiana were also considered Creole.

The Creole ruling class led a revolt, known as the Insurrection of 1768, and sent the Spanish governor packing. Spain responded by sending Governor O'Reilly to rule the colony; he was a determined leader who brought with him two thousand troops and twenty ships. He reoccupied New Orleans without firing a shot, publicly executed the leaders of the revolt by firing squad, and imprisoned and confiscated the property of others who had participated.[20]

Though initially resistant to Spanish rule, Creoles soon discovered that Spain meant to invest money in the colony and to send competent administrators who would establish Louisiana as a stable, growing outpost. Under Spain's governance, Louisiana evolved from a sparsely settled military buffer zone into a dynamic commercial center. Spain governed Louisiana but did not colonize it. The Spanish gave Creole Louisianans significant autonomy, did not rob them of their language, and in many ways maintained the cultural status quo. Though Spanish in name, the colony remained culturally French, and most Spanish officials assimilated through intermarriage and adopted French Creole customs. Trade increased both upriver to the newly settled American West and downriver through the Gulf of Mexico to the Caribbean and Europe.

A plantation economy developed, with cotton and sugar replacing indigo and tobacco as major cash crops. Spain brought in thousands of enslaved Africans, dramatically expanding slavery and further contributing to the creation of a plantation system. Along with the increased population of enslaved Africans, Louisiana experienced renewed immigration from Acadian exiles, Canary Islanders, and refugees from the slave revolts in St. Domingue, present-day Haiti.

In the late eighteenth century, Louisiana underwent a re-Africanization of the enslaved population. In 1766, the enslaved population was less than six thousand, but by 1788 it had surged to more than twenty thousand. This exponential increase in forced African migration transformed the economy and culture of Louisiana. African music, drumming, dancing, and languages flourished.[21] Under the Spanish, the enslaved experienced a more liberal system than the regulations imposed by the French Code Noir. Enslaved people could hold mass meetings at Congo Square in New

Orleans, lodge complaints against abusive masters, and engage in a system of self-purchase known as *coartación*. Manumission, the emancipation of a slave, was more accessible, resulting in 2–4 percent of the enslaved population being freed each year. This led to a whole new caste in Louisiana society. Known as *gens de couleur libres* (free people of color) they worked as laborers and skilled craftsmen and numbered 1,500 by 1803. By 1810, they comprised one-quarter of the city's population. Most of the free people of color in New Orleans were women, many of whom partnered with men of wholly European ancestry. In his study of free people of color in the South, Warren E. Milteer noted, "Although the laws of the South gave their relationships no sanction, free people of color and their white partners challenged the very existence of an indelible color line in the South."[22]

American settlers were drawn to the burgeoning prosperity and growth in Louisiana. By 1795, the United States was granted the right to navigate the Mississippi River and deposit goods in New Orleans. After Napoleon briefly reacquired Louisiana from Spain, the United States saw its chance and offered him money he desperately needed to finance his military campaigns in exchange for the suddenly viable, wealthy colony.

The Americans acquired a colony accustomed to monarchal rule yet determined to maintain its autonomy. The social order that emerged from the French and Spanish colonial eras was contrary to that of the old regime of Europe. Nobility and royal connections did not determine prestige and success. Instead, the ownership of land, slaveholding, and established kinship networks dictated who were members of the ruling class. At the time of the Louisiana Purchase in 1803, the colony had become firmly rooted in a slave-based plantation system controlled by an elite Creole planter-merchant class. A three-caste racial system characterized a still somewhat unstable society.

The purchase of Louisiana by the United States brought massive political and legal changes and social unrest. The *ancienne population,* or established Creole elite, spoke French and was accustomed to imperial rule and a feudal mindset. The arriving Americans spoke English, embraced democracy, and engaged in an individualistic, free-enterprise system. The Creoles were Catholic, and the Americans belonged to Protestant denominations. The new legal code combined elements of both civil law (French and Spanish) and common law (Anglo-American).

The Creoles opposed many changes brought by the Americans, including republican government, the common-law system, and a social order that favored equality more than class. They wanted local autonomy and were against federal control, as they fought to maintain their power and their culture. However, Creoles embraced the Americans' goals of prosperity, growth, and maintenance of a racial order. With the invention of the cotton gin and a discovery of a means of granulating sugar, large-scale plantation agriculture began to dominate the state. New Orleans achieved global significance, becoming the fourth busiest commercial port in the western world by 1840. The once-isolated colony dependent on a frontier exchange economy became a state with a credit-based economy dominated by agriculture and exports.[23]

The tripartite racial caste system was able to survive for so long in Louisiana because of the power struggle between Creoles and Americans. Free people of color, predominantly Francophone Catholics, helped maintain Creole population numbers and bolstered their cultural hold. White Creoles and Creoles of color could form an unlikely, unequal, and uneasy alliance when their dominance was challenged by Anglo-Americans. Thus, the tripartite racial caste system actually benefited Creoles in the years before the Civil War.

Louisiana's population boomed, increasing ninefold between 1810 and 1830. Americans flocked to the new state. Immigrants from Ireland, Germany, and other European nations arrived at the port of New Orleans and made their home in the bustling city. Even the predominantly Creole and African enslaved population saw a transformation. The United States ended slave importation from Africa in 1808. Louisiana's plantations still had unmet labor needs, so the Americans launched a massive interstate domestic slave trade. Slaves from the Upper South—Virginia, North and South Carolina, and Maryland—were sold to traders and brought on ships or in coffles to Louisiana and other neighboring Deep South states. In what became known as the second Middle Passage, approximately one million enslaved individuals were sold away from their families and homes. New

Orleans soon became North America's largest slave market.[24] The American slaves arrived on Louisiana plantations speaking English and worshiping as Baptists or Methodists. They intermarried with French-speaking, Catholic Creole slaves, changing the cultural landscape of the area.

When Louisiana achieved statehood in 1812, Creoles and Americans both believed that slavery was essential to the state's prosperity. Under the Americans, slavery was not only a system of economic exploitation but also developed into a means of racial control. When the Spanish ruled Louisiana, laws governing slavery were not as harsh, emancipation was accessible, and racial distinctions were less rigid. Wealthy Creoles, now owners of plantations dependent on a vast slave workforce, joined with Americans to reject the Spanish system, which they deemed lax and overly tolerant. Disturbed by the dominance of people of color on the levee, in the markets, on street corners, and in public houses, wealthy Creoles and Americans believed that white and Black people should not be allowed to interact as if they were equal. They began to enact restrictions on slaves and free people of color. New Orleans's evolution from a frontier outpost to a metropolis involved significant changes in cultural norms.

Although the legislature was at first dominated by Creoles, many embraced the Americans' adherence to a strict racial order and passed oppressive slave laws more in keeping with Anglo-American common law than French and Spanish civil law. Creoles and Americans worked together to control slave labor, keep slaves enslaved, and protect the rights of property holders. All that remained un-Americanized was the three-tiered racial system—whites, slaves, and free people of color—left over from the French and Spanish eras. It would be challenged in the decades leading up to the Civil War. Ultimately free people of color were stripped of their rights, and emancipation became illegal by 1857.[25]

Despite their ability to prosper and adapt, free people of color in Louisiana always endured restrictions on their freedom. According to the Louisiana Civil Code of 1808, free people of color were required to have the initials "f.p.c." (free person of color), "f.m.c." (free man of color), or "f.w.c." (free woman of color) after their names in all legal documents. The law code forbade free people of color from marrying whites. For two decades, illegitimate or natural-born children could inherit from their white fathers if these fathers had acknowledged them in notarized legal documents. By 1828, however, the law was changed to deny mixed-race children the right to inherit under any circumstances. H. M. St. Paul, a state senator for Orleans Parish, summed up the prevalent viewpoint of white Creoles and Americans toward free people of color: "Oh! But we are told that some of them are rich—some of them are fair, scarce a characteristic of the African origin remaining. What if they Be? . . . Does it therefore follow that we are to recognize their social equality, invite them to our homes, and give our children to them in marriage? Never! Never!"[26]

Many of the individuals profiled in this book were deemed natural-born children. Because it was illegal for enslaved women and free women of color to marry white men, any children born to these unions would be considered natural born, which essentially meant illegitimate. Even if acknowledged by their fathers, they could not automatically be emancipated, and children had to reach a certain age before the manumission became legal. Freeing the enslaved became an increasingly rigorous process that, by 1857, was unattainable. Even if their fathers considered these natural-born children their own, they could not inherit property because of their race and illegitimacy.

Invisible Blackness explores the complex lives of Creoles of mixed race who shared the same language, religion, blood, and culture as their white cousins but never the same status. This book examines the ways these natural children, born of enslaved women and the white men who owned them, chose to reinvent themselves and forge their own identities within the increasingly strict racial order of antebellum and post–Civil War Louisiana. Its scope includes both the traditionally studied plantation settings and urban spaces in New Orleans, the largest city in the South during the period studied. A vast array of records collected over twenty years of research, including sacramental, vital, and notarial records; bills of sale; successions; wills; and military pension files, shed light on how this liminal group defined itself and ultimately how its members shaped their own identities.

Historian Marisa J. Fuentes's argument that archives do not contain voices of the enslaved and thus commit "violence" against them holds some merit; researching the lives of enslaved women is extremely challenging, and discovering instances where they discuss the brutality of what they endured can be close to impossible. However, I counter this notion of archives as spaces of "violence" by noting that they hold the only evidence available to us; when an experienced researcher works with dedicated archivists, archives can yield incredible insights into the lives of enslaved women. Archival documents, recorded oral histories, legal records, and newspaper accounts remain our only hope of arriving at any degree of understanding of the past. Rather than vilifying archives, we must recognize that the white supremacist patriarchal system is at fault. We can acknowledge how this has affected what documents remain and how they have been interpreted without dismissing or demonizing the archive.[27]

This work examines the lives of Alice Thomasson Grice, her children, and friends of mixed racial heritage. Their individual lives form the center of the narrative, and stories of their family, friends, and community radiate from their experiences. Alice's story is unique, because her father considered her formerly enslaved mother to be his wife, and she and her siblings were raised as free people. Charles Grice, a white steamboat captain, married Alice and legitimized their children, and the family chose to identify as white. This work explores why Alice, her children, and her friends Marguerite Grossinger and Georgina Gaal chose to cross the color line during the era that historian Joel Williamson deemed "the age of passing," roughly spanning the years between 1880 and 1925. The rate of passing corresponded with the severity of oppression and discrimination toward Blacks in the South.

By the 1890s, at the height of violent racial tensions nationally—when Jim Crow laws were affirmed by the Supreme Court, establishing segregation as the rule of the day, and lynchings were on the rise—people of color who could pass had strong motivations to do so. Determining the exact number of people who crossed this taboo boundary is challenging; it was an act that was inherently meant to be shrouded in secrecy, hidden, and, if possible, undocumented. Best estimates indicate that the Grices were among 110,000 people with African ancestry identifying as white across the United States, with a rate of between 2,500 to 2,750 people "passing over" per year. In Louisiana, with its high population of mixed-race individuals, it is probable that between 100 and 500 people of color "became white" every year from 1875 to the 1890s.

What contributed to Louisiana's exceptionalism? These are the very factors we think of today when we compare Louisiana, particularly New Orleans, to the rest of the nation: the civil rather than common-law legal system, a French-language heritage, predominance of the Catholic faith, and Latin social mores. Because of its French and Spanish colonial roots, Louisiana has always been more closely related to the Caribbean than to the rest of the United States, both culturally and in the way that ideas about race evolved. People are quick to point out that other urban areas had populations of free people of color. However, none resembled New Orleans. In her study of free people of color in Charleston, Amrita Myers pointed out that Charleston's free people of color were denied access to "white collar professions" and "often had ceilings imposed on their wages." This was never the case in New Orleans; in fact, many free people of color in New Orleans possessed significant wealth. Myers noted that more enslaved individuals—and significantly more enslaved women—engaged in self-purchase in New Orleans. After the Louisiana Purchase, Americans were stunned that free people of color owned more than one-quarter of the properties lining New Orleans's main thoroughfares. Unlike in the rest of the South, men in New Orleans were open about their relationships with women of color and frequently acknowledged their biracial children. "The reticence of Charleston's slaveowners about their sex lives was also common," Myers wrote. "While interracial sex occurred in all slave centers in the United States, only in New Orleans was it accepted and legitimated by the individuals, the church, and the courts."

Shockingly most scholarly works about passing and interracial relationships fail to even include Louisiana, the place that was the epicenter of these experiences, likely because Louisiana proves exceptional. These researchers, primarily professors of English and history, would have had to familiarize themselves with the civil-law system, engage in serious archival work translating documents from French and Spanish, and explore a tripartite racial system and culture that would essentially be foreign to them. Although their reluctance to include Louisiana is understandable, the fact that they do not even address the exclusion is significant and unfortunate. This is true for the works of Allyson Hobbs, Alisha Gaines, and Michelle Elam. In *That Middle World: Race, Performance, and the Politics of Passing*, Julia S. Charles only mentions Louisiana in one paragraph about *Plessy v. Ferguson*. She noted that Plessy "boarded a train in Louisiana—a state with a hierarchical racial structure somewhat different from that of the rest of the nation." Hobbs also alluded to Plessy and gave a few pages to P. B. S. Pinchback, a Louisiana politician born in Mississippi and raised in Cincinnati; neither of these men ever crossed the color line. None of these authors give any attention to Creoles. The exclusion of Louisiana from recent historical narratives that address passing is a serious failure in scholarship. This subject will never be fully understood until Louisiana is included.[28]

After the Civil War, Louisiana began to move toward the binary racial hierarchy present in the rest of the South. As a result, a significant number of Creoles found themselves in an "Americanized" society in which they no longer had a place. They were forced to make difficult decisions about how they defined themselves. By the early twentieth century, the Grices and their friends no longer had a choice: a war for "racial purity" was being waged by government officials and people in positions of power, and nuance and tolerance were no longer acceptable.

Invisible Blackness has several aims. Within these pages, I discuss the unique cultural heritage of Louisiana, the more fluid approach to racial identification that has always existed here, and how ideas of race evolved over time. I explore the notion of "passing," race as a social construct, and what it means to be a family. There are implications in this study that are applicable to the broader American narrative. More than anything else, I hope that the lives of Marguerite, Alice, and their friends compel you to question what we have been taught in our history classes and what we want our children to learn in the future. I hope their stories move you as much as they have me. When confronted with the "point" of these pages, I must be clear: this has very little to do with the abstract philosophies and intellectual jargon of the ivory towers of academia and everything to do with the fact that I found Marguerite and Alice, believed their lives mattered—and still matter—and that the world should once again say their names. It is my hope that in learning about them, you will learn more about yourself and your ideas about race, class, history, and family.

Historian and writer Marcus Christian, in an unpublished manuscript written in 1960s New Orleans, wrote, "New Orleans . . . has given to America—north and south—more 'passe pour blanches' than any other city in our country. That term . . . means literally, 'people who pass for white.' And this is no exaggeration, for it is there that family lines waver back and forth across color lines like wet wash on a windy March day."[29] For families like the Grices, only fractionally Black and physically appearing white, passing afforded the only means of social, economic, and political advancement available to them. Complexion, education, finances, and family all influenced the decision to identify as white. Ultimately these natural children had a choice: they could redefine and create their own identities because of the diversity of their background. Their lives underscore that race is a social construct and yet also a very significant aspect of an individual's reality. Beyond these broad pressing historical questions lie issues of love, family, and the universal quest for belonging that transcends time, place, and race.

PROLOGUE

On the west bank of the nation's mightiest river in the nation, fifty miles upriver from the city of New Orleans, a baby girl was born into slavery. Yet she would soon know freedom. Those were the days when the Spanish ruled the land, and manumission was a common practice. Her father Christophe Haydel, the man who owned her, and her mother Angelique, the enslaved mulatto woman he held in bondage, called her Seraphine.[1] At the time of her birth, she was not legally entitled to a surname, but that would soon change.

On May 27, 1795, Christophe Haydel, one of the most successful plantation owners in St. John the Baptist Parish, took steps to ensure that his children of color would have a future beyond the fields that surrounded them. He knew that, on his death, his white children with his legal wife would each receive land and slaves. His daughter Magdelaine Haydel Becnel, a grown adult and married woman at the time of his death, would inherit and run his plantation for the rest of her life.[2] But it was also important to him that his daughter Seraphine and her siblings Simphorien, Celeste, and Eugenie would be more than property that his white children would inherit. So, he sold three-year-old Seraphine and her siblings, described as "four young quadroons," to their Aunt Charlotte, who had already been freed, with the stipulation that she must grant them their freedom and that they must live with their mother, a twenty-eight-year-old mulatto woman named Angelique. That same day he declared Angelique legally free on his death and the death of his wife.[3]

Seraphine grew up in the French Quarter home of first her aunt and then her mother.[4] She gave birth to her first child when she was around fifteen years old. When the priest at St. Louis Cathedral was to perform the child's baptism, he asked Seraphine for her surname.[5] She became known as Seraphine Christophe, adopting her father's first name as her last, a common Creole practice. Later when she became a woman of property, engaging in the buying and selling of real estate and enslaved people, she used the name Haydel.[6] She was by no means the only Haydel woman involved in business. Her half-sister Magdelaine Haydel Becnel turned the farm where they had been born into a prosperous sugar plantation known today as Evergreen. At her death, Magdelaine left a legacy for her descendants; the plantation would pass into the hands of first her grandson, then great-grandson, and finally her great-great-grandchildren. Even though Seraphine was a free woman of color and seemingly limited by that status, her children and grandchildren would also benefit both from her connections and her fortune. Both Haydel women became the matriarchs of strong and illustrious families.

Evergreen Plantation, birthplace of Seraphine Haydel. Photograph copyright © Mfmegevand | Dreamstime.com.

Seraphine began a relationship with Achille Rivarde, a French-speaking Creole like herself. The couple would certainly have married but were prohibited by law from doing so because they were of different races. At least eight children were born to the Rivardes, four of whom survived to adulthood.[7] Rivarde, a wealthy merchant, fell on hard times after the financial crisis of 1837 and struggled to rebound. Fearing that his property might be seized to cover his debts and aware that Seraphine and their children could not legally inherit from him, Rivarde began transferring property to them. In 1845, he sold eleven enslaved men, women, and children to her along with a plot of land.[8] One year later, Rivarde and his business partner "mysteriously disappeared," having left a letter "stating that heavy losses he had experienced had rendered him unable to meet his obligations, and not being able to survive his misfortunes, he was determined to put an end to his life."[9] What might have started as a ruse ultimately resulted in his actual demise. His funeral took place at his Esplanade Street home on March 28, 1848.[10]

Achille Rivarde's end was certainly tragic for his family, but he was able to see at least one of his daughters settled before his death. All three of his daughters made good matches, but perhaps the best of all was achieved by Elisabeth. She wed Joseph Dumas on February 24, 1831, at St. Louis Cathedral, surrounded by family that included her Uncle Firmin, her brother, and Achille Rivarde, whom the priest identified as her father in the marriage ledger.[11] A free man of color and successful tailor, Joseph Dumas partnered with Julien Clovis to amass vast holdings of commercial real estate. His trade may have been that of a tailor, but the means of his rise to wealth and power was acquiring property.[12] He became so prosperous that he decided to move his family to France, where the Dumas's six children were raised.[13] Life in Paris for the Dumas family proved infinitely superior to New Orleans, where despite their wealth and status they would always exist as second-class citizens. Meanwhile Seraphine remained in New Orleans with her daughter Anais, living in a home on Ursulines in the Tremé that Joseph Dumas had sold her.[14]

It seemed the Dumas family would go on living in exile in Paris, content and comfortable. Yet the fortune that financed their lifestyle was dependent on Joseph Dumas's holdings in Louisiana, which required some maintenance and oversight. Rising to the challenge, his son François Ernest Dumas returned to his ancestral home in 1860, just in time to bid his grandmother farewell: Seraphine Rivarde, as she was then known, died at her home in the Tremé on August 21, 1860.[15] Dumas had spent five years at university in Paris. Almost at the same time and under the same circumstances—having studied for several years in Paris—Michel Becnel, a great-great-grandson of Seraphine's half-sister Magdelaine, also returned home to Louisiana.[16] Michel and his brother began to run their plantation while Dumas handled his family's business in New Orleans, all as rumblings of war were overtaking the nation.

With the coming of the Civil War, New Orleans, the largest city in the Confederacy and a major port, became an important target for the U.S. Army and Navy. Despite the significance of New Orleans, the Confederacy chose to focus on Virginia and areas in the Upper South, leaving the Crescent City with limited resources to defend itself from capture. In April 1862, the U.S. Navy succeeded in overcoming the forts below New Orleans and soon steamed up the Mississippi River and took the city. Confederate troops then retreated into the interior of the state. Plans were made for U.S. forces to pursue them, and gunboats were sent upriver. Rumors began circulating that Confederates might try to attack New Orleans, and reports of Confederate fighting in the River Parishes outside New Orleans raised fears. General Benjamin Butler, in charge of New Orleans, became open to the possibility of Black men enlisting in the U.S. Army. While the city was still under Confederate control, free men of color had formed militia groups ostensibly loyal to that cause. However, the vast majority did so only under severe pressure; the state legislature had been systematically stripping these free men of their rights, and the threat of repercussions and even of violence if they did not comply was uppermost in the minds of free people of color when they formed the Louisiana Native Guard. After negotiations, the Louisiana Native Guard became the first Black unit to serve in the U.S. Army during the Civil War.[17]

Francis Dumas, as he was now called, having adopted an Americanized version of his name, proved instrumental to the Louisiana Native

Guard's decision to join the fight for freedom. Although many white U.S. soldiers did not yet believe that they had taken up arms to free enslaved people, the free men of color of New Orleans had the foresight to see that such action was inevitable. They had spent their lives watching their rights shrink and being denied the dignity they merited. They inherently understood that taking up arms against white Confederates, many of whom were their own relatives, would be the only way that they would ever attain equal rights before the law. Dumas used his influence and fortune to enable the formation of the first Black regiments. "I raised myself Company B of the 1st La [Native Guard] of which I was commissioned a captain and afterward I was promoted by Maj. Gen. Butler as major of the 2d. La. [Native Guard]," he wrote. "No one in the community can doubt that we were active [sic] by true patriotism and without interest."[18] General Butler called Dumas "a man who would be worth a quarter of a million dollars in reasonably good times" and noted that he spoke three languages in addition to French and English. Clearly impressed with Dumas, Butler noted, "He had more capability as a Major than I had as Major General, I am quite sure."[19]

Much has been made of the possibility that Dumas enslaved people. Some newspapers even erroneously reported that he owned a plantation and freed his slaves so they could fight in the Native Guard. This was simply not true. Dumas was the son of a businessman who maintained only an urban residence. Dumas's grandfather Achille Rivarde did sell enslaved people to Joseph Dumas and his daughter Elisabeth Rivarde Dumas. Most were enslaved women and their children who worked as domestics within their household. Yet according to the slave schedule of 1850, by that year the Joseph Dumas family only enslaved one woman. There has not been a single document found that indicates that Francis E. Dumas enslaved anyone. No evidence supports other fabricated claims, which were based solely on newspaper reports that were not fact checked.[20] Meanwhile Seraphine Rivarde's half-sister's family, the Becnels of Evergreen Plantation, enslaved more than one hundred people at the beginning of the Civil War.[21] The Becnel brothers soon answered the call of the Confederacy. Both were serving as captains in the Confederate Army when New Orleans fell.[22]

U.S. military officers were amazed and entranced by Dumas and his family and circle of friends. In September 1862, Captain John William deForest attended a party at the home of Dumas's brother, where he was entertained in high Creole fashion. English mingled with French at a supper of "cakes, confectionery, creams, ices, and champagne, followed by café noir, cognac, and delicious cigars." Afterward, a piano accompanied the singing of both French and American patriotic tunes and then dancing to waltzes and polkas. DeForest described Dumas as having "the complexion of an Italian and features which remind one of the first Napoleon." The young American officer came away knowing that he had encountered a unique culture, unlike any he had witnessed in the rest of the country. "I saw last evening something very curious and interesting to me," he wrote. "I saw a new race; a race which is seeking to win a respectable footing in human society; a race which holds such a footing in Europe though scorned by us." The Creoles of color of New Orleans made a lasting impression on him.[23]

In the autumn of 1862, the Second Louisiana Native Guard, commanded by Colonel Nathan Daniels and Major Francis Dumas, was sent to guard the railroad and to suppress guerilla attacks along the Mississippi River in St. John the Baptist and St. James Parishes. When they received reports of Confederates near Vacherie, Louisiana, Daniels and Dumas took Company B to investigate. They arrived at the Duparc & Locoul Plantation at the height of the harvest. The enslaved workers out in the sugarcane fields dropped their machetes at the sight of them. Later that evening, Daniels and Dumas were invited into the home of the plantation owner Flagy Duparc, who entertained the U.S. officers in his dining room. He treated them with courtesy and offered them wine. Yet according to Dumas, an issue did arise. "He found only one fault with me," Dumas reminisced, "which was being a Creole, born in Louisiana, that I was in the Yankee Army."[24] Duparc considered himself and Dumas to be of the same culture and heritage, despite being of different races, and he could not understand why Dumas would take up arms against his own people.

Soon after their arrival in Vacherie, Daniels received orders to encamp in the area and establish himself as provost marshal for the region. He consulted with his major regarding the best-situated place to do so. They marched down the River Road to a plantation owned by captains in the Confederate Army, now run by an overseer in the absence of the masters. Major Dumas, the highest-ranking Black man in the army of the United States of America, stood before the plantation on which his grandmother had been born a slave. Whether it was he or Daniels who made the call remains a mystery. The plantation founded by Christophe Haydel, Dumas's great-grandfather, became the headquarters of the Second Louisiana Native Guard.[25]

A few days later a woman came to the camp, brought there by Louis Smith, Flagy Duparc's enslaved coachman, at the request of Colonel Daniels. She was a Creole woman who had been raised Catholic and spoke French, just like Francis Dumas, then in charge of the camp where she stood, and Michel Becnel, the man who owned the plantation. Like Dumas, she appeared white but was of mixed racial ancestry. Yet she had never known the freedom of Dumas or Becnel. She had been born into slavery and remained in that condition until Dumas and Daniels appeared on the scene. Her name was Marguerite. This is her story and the story of her most intimate friends and acquaintances.[26]

1

THE ISSUE OF HER BODY

Alice Thomasson

Alice Thomasson likely spent Christmas Eve of 1858 monitoring the weather; the local newspaper lamented that "Christmas itself came in weepingly."[1] Christmas Eve's raw cold and wind left business on the levee so slow that Charles Grice could come home early to celebrate. Business would pick up again on the docks once the holiday passed and the weather improved.[2] Later in the day, a wind came up that dried off the wet banquettes, and shoppers took to the streets, gazing into the glittering shop windows, dazzled by the holiday displays. By 10:00 o'clock that evening, the gloomy sky glowed from the light of a faraway fire, a Christmas Eve bonfire in Algiers, just across the river from where Alice's family lived.[3] She and Charles shared his rented lodgings on Gasquet Street in a neighborhood just beginning to be developed.[4]

As clerk on the steamboat *Natchez,* Charles was essentially its business manager. He kept the accounts, worked with merchants, sold tickets, and assigned rooms. He was responsible for the cargo and making sure it was all aboard and paid for.[5] His position was crucial to the success of the steamboat's trip up the Mississippi, and his captain, known for his punctuality and professionalism, would be expecting him soon. Charles Grice was among the most elite steamboat officers on the river. "Nothing tends more to render a boat popular than to have good officers, prompt, correct, and courteous gentlemen," the *Picayune* reported when the *Natchez*

The *Natchez* as Charles Grice knew it. Steamboat Images, MS 1052. LSU Libraries, Louisiana and Lower Mississippi Valley Collections.

resumed its regular schedule in September after its summer break. "Such the *Natchez* has . . . everybody knows them . . . as officers, they have no superior."[6] The *Natchez* departed New Orleans promptly at five o'clock in the evening every Saturday, stopping at the main ports and river landings along the way, until it reached Vicksburg, where it would dock until its scheduled Tuesday departure.[7] Charles would have said goodbye to Alice, whom he would see again at the end of the week, and made his way downtown toward the riverfront.

The Vieux Carré was crowded with holiday revelers and visitors intent on enjoying the entertainments of the season. The Opera House and the St. Charles Hotel offered programs that evening, and the Amphitheatre was set to showcase gymnasts, acrobats, and clowns. The hotels were full to bursting with travelers, many of whom Charles had transported or seen arrive at the wharf.[8] Once aboard the *Natchez*, the elite passengers would dine on a fourteen-course Christmas dinner, with a bill of fare of four kinds of fish, six broiled meats, six varieties of roasts, eight entrées, nine cold dishes, five types of game, and thirty-six desserts. The lavish dinner would be served on silverware, china, and linens made especially for "the monarch of boats."[9] Yet that evening his attention was likely on matters other than the grandeur before him.

Alice and Charles had received a Christmas gift, the knowledge that Alice was expecting their first child: although not unwelcome, it presented complications. Then around seventeen years old, Alice was eight years younger than Charles, who was orphaned at a young age and had been fending for himself as a river boatman for years. Yet neither age, experience, nor socioeconomic status was a problematic factor in their relationship in that time and place. Charles, a steamboat clerk, was the son of a steamboat captain, and Alice's father and uncle were steamboat captains as well. Both Charles and Alice had received comparable educations; in fact, her signature was finer than his. However, despite a seeming lack of impediments and their commitment to each other, they could never legally marry. Under current Louisiana law, Alice would never be considered Charles's wife, and the child they were expecting would be deemed illegitimate at birth. Though the shoppers and theatergoers braving the cold of New Orleans's wet streets that evening would never have been able to tell, Alice was technically a woman of color. The state of Louisiana recognized her legal status as that of colored, and no matter her complexion or appearance, she was deemed Black and therefore legally forbidden from entering into marriage with a white man. Though she was now living as a free woman of color in New Orleans, Alice had come perilously close to being permanently enslaved in the cane fields of Lafourche Parish.

In the late 1820s, Alexander Thomasson, a young man from Pointe Coupée Parish trying to make his way in the world, traveled downriver to the Lafourche region and settled in the small village of Thibodaux.[10] His father had left France for Louisiana in the latter half of the previous century, and though his surname was frequently confused with the Anglo "Thompson," the family's origins were Gallic.[11] One of his brothers, Ferriol, was a middle-class planter in West Feliciana Parish; the other, St. Clair, sought his fortune on the river, becoming the captain of a steamboat.[12] Alexander partnered with another new arrival to Thibodaux and tried his hand at the grocery business but failed to make a go of it. After that, perhaps inspired by the increased river traffic with the advent of the steamboat, he oversaw the construction of a large building and stables in Thibodaux, believing he could use them to run a boarding house and barroom. Yet again he met with failure, and he soon became "disgusted of his former occupation." Mounting debts and limited credit forced him to take out several promissory notes from a well-to-do neighbor, seeing that as the only option remaining to him. Alexander was determined to buy a steamboat and become a captain like his brother. In fact, he probably gained experience working on a steamboat because of St. Clair's position. Around 1834 or 1835, Alexander became captain of the steamboat *Paul Jones* and, a few years later, of the *Teche*.[13]

Steamboats were not the only property he acquired. In June 1831, Alexander came into possession of Milly, an eighteen-year-old enslaved woman of mixed race. Though the man who enslaved her, William Schaeffer, a nearby plantation owner, did not originally want to sell her, Alexander persisted and finally a purchase price of $600 was agreed on. Over the course of the next decade, Milly had several children, increasing her value as property.

By the fall of 1839, Alexander's debts and financial mismanagement caught up to him yet again. Henry Claiborne Thibodaux, the man who had loaned him money, approached him for payment. Alexander first evaded him, then would not honor the promissory notes, and "altogether neglected and refused to pay." Thibodaux took Alexander to court for $5,859.75 plus interest owed to him from notes issued in December 1836 and July and December 1838. Keenly aware that Alexander had no cash or assets, Thibodaux went after him for property that, though technically not his, he had maintained ownership of—the lot and building in Thibodaux and the enslaved woman Milly and her children. At the courthouse in Thibodaux, Alexander, his brother St. Clair, and his sister Marie Azelie Cook were accused of pretending to sell the property to protect it from seizure to cover Alexander's debts. The evidence presented to the court left little doubt, presenting a chain of dubious property sales by the Thomasson siblings. Alexander had sold his lot and building to his sisters, Marie A. and Eugenie Thomasson, on March 19, 1830, for $2,500. A little more than a year later, Eugenie sold her half of the property to Marie Azelie, now wife of George Cook, for $1,200. St. Clair ultimately purchased the property from Marie A. Cook on February 27, 1834, for $4,000. All the while, Alexander remained in possession of the property, lived in the building, and acted as owner, even paying taxes on it.

Milly's ownership was also questionable. A perusal of courthouse records revealed that Alexander's name was not on the bill of sale; instead, his sister Marie Azelie claimed to have purchased the enslaved woman from William Schaeffer and insisted that Milly had in fact been her property, not her brother's. Marie Azelie then sold Milly to St. Clair on February 25, 1834. Yet Thibodaux persisted, claiming that in fact Marie Azelie Thomasson Cook and St. Clair were "falsely named as purchaser[s]" and that Milly was "in truth sold to Alexander" in a conspiracy entered into by the siblings with an "intent to shelter the said slave from pursuit of the said Alexander Thomasson's Creditors, and to defraud petitioner of his eventual right upon the said slave and her issue." Because Alexander had no other property to settle the debt, Thibodaux demanded that the court order the seizure and sale of the lot and building, as well as Milly and her children.

The local court dismissed the suit. It found in favor of the Thomassons, claiming that no creditor can "sue individually to annul any contract made before the time of his debt accrued." Thibodaux could not individually annul contracts entered into by the Thomassons, and these contracts, dating years prior to Alexander's debt with Thibodaux, should not be broken. Thibodaux, however, was undeterred by the court's ruling: he filed an appeal, and the case was again brought to trial.

This time testimony was taken from the Thomasson siblings, as well as various witnesses familiar with Alexander. St. Clair Thomasson denied all allegations. Marie and George Cook testified that all sales had been bona fide. Yet the other witnesses contradicted them, stating that St. Clair had never occupied the property in Thibodaux, that Alexander had always presented himself as owner and even had attempted to sell the lot and building to them, and that Milly had always been in Alexander's possession. Peter Walsh, one of the witnesses, recounted a conversation with St. Clair: "He had suffered his brother [Alexander] to remain in possession of the property, that he had run him to immense expense by making improvements thereon, which he said would enhance its value, that he however, saw that it was useless to expect any profit from it, and wished to dispose, if possible of the property." It was becoming increasingly clear that Alexander had sought his siblings' help in masking his troubles and protecting his property from seizure to pay off his mounting debts. St. Clair, Marie, and Eugenie must have shared a strong bond with their brother to have gone to such trouble, allowing themselves to become embroiled in lawsuits and questionable dealings on his behalf. The eldest brother, Ferriol, at the time the wealthiest of the siblings with land and slaves several parishes upriver, had not involved himself in his younger brother's troubles.

The testimony of William Schaeffer, Milly's former owner, not only questioned the validity of the sale under question but also revealed details about Alexander's relationship with Milly. He found the circumstances of her sale to be unusual. Milly had run away from the plantation, and when Schaeffer went in search of her, he found her in Alexander's kitchen. Schaeffer told the court that he "thought [Alexander] had induced her to run away and concealed her." This was a serious charge for which Alexander could have been prosecuted. What would motivate Alexander to shelter a runaway slave despite the harsh penalties for doing so? According to Schaeffer, Alexander "wished to buy her for the purpose of keeping her as a mistress." He had found Milly with what appeared to be special presents from Alexander: "a strange cloak and umbrella." Discovering her asleep in his kitchen further confirmed his suspicions that Alexander had pursued a relationship with her and induced her to run away. He "manifested great anxiety to purchase the slave," yet he was unable to pay the necessary $600. When the time came for the sale, Alexander requested that it be done in his sister's name. Schaeffer continued to see Milly with Alexander Thomasson, even though she was ostensibly his sister's property. Schaeffer vacillated a bit at the end of his testimony, possibly nervous about his serious accusations, stating that he "has no personal knowledge of intercourse between the slave Milly and Alex Thomasson. Report was that Thomasson kept her."

Milly's children, "the issue of her body," were also Alexander Thomasson's. Born of a white father and a mother who was classified in the racial descriptor of the time as a mulatto, they were considered quadroons, of one-quarter African descent. One of these children was Alice, who would grow up to be a woman walking freely down the streets of New Orleans, yet still restricted in her liberties and incapable of marrying the man she loved. Her situation paralleled that of her parents.

Ultimately the jury decided that the acts of sale between the Thomassons were "false, fraudulent, and simulated." The district court ordered that the lot and the slave Milly and her children "be seized and sold" and that the proceeds from the sale would be applied to the debt Alexander owed to Thibodaux. St. Clair objected to the ruling and filed an appeal that came before the Louisiana Supreme Court, which affirmed the judgment rendered by the district court: Alice, her mother, and siblings would have to be sold to cover her father's debts. Under such circumstances, she could find herself laboring in the cane fields in just a few years, possibly separated from her family and certainly removed from her father. Alexander and Milly's family would be inextricably dissolved, and there was nothing that Alexander could do to protect the woman he considered his wife and the children he loved.

Curiously the Supreme Court's decision ended with this statement: "The questions of law, which the present appellant has urged, were considered and disposed of, when this case was before us between the plaintiff and some of the co-defendants of the appellant." It appears that the debt had been settled before the seizure and sale of Milly and the children, probably by Alexander's brother St. Clair. The family remained intact for now.

Alexander Thomasson dodged past carpetbag-carrying travelers, loaded drays, and stacks of barrels and boxes. After twenty years on the river, the burning resin and pitch pine didn't so much as make him cough. The black smoke rising from the towering smokestacks along the wharves spread across the city, a sign that the afternoon departure of the steamboats was only a few hours away. He approached the deck of the *Magnolia*, his brother's magnificent steamboat that over the last few years had developed a reputation as "one of the most superb, swift and commodious steamers upon the Mississippi."[14] The *Magnolia* transported both cotton and passengers from New Orleans to Vicksburg and was the largest cotton boat of its day. When the cotton season ended, usually in the spring and early summer, the *Magnolia* carried the most elite passengers on the river up to vacation destinations like Louisville and even Niagara Falls. St. Clair's success was evident the moment Alexander stepped on deck and walked through the splendid boat with staterooms full of "the best class of passengers at a price that few other boats presumed to charge." Guests would not soon forget their time on the *Magnolia*, with its "sumptuous fare" and elegant service.[15] Yet Alexander was not there to admire his brother's boat but to seek his help in saving his own. Embroiled in yet another court case, he turned once again to St. Clair, who had become a legend in New Orleans and all upriver ports.[16]

Captain St. Clair Thomasson, a lifelong bachelor and successful businessman with a larger-than-life personality, was considered "the most noted of all the captains on the Father of Waters."[17] Some accounts said he was born to an American and a French woman; others declared the reverse. At times decidedly of "creole birth" and on other occasions a suave "Frenchman," St. Clair inhabited the American world of commerce and industry while still maintaining the charm, elegance, and aristocratic demeanor of the French Creole, particularly with his female passengers.[18] A Turkish naval captain, struck by St. Clair's kindness and skill, believed it his duty to submit a letter of commendation to the Louisville newspaper expressing the high esteem in which he held his Mississippi River captain. "Speaking French as well as English," Captain Zerman noted, "Capt.

Thomasson has blended, in a charming manner, on his steamer, American and European manners."[19]

His manners were not the only aspect of his life that was blended; his brother Alexander considered his mulatto slave his wife and recognized their children as his own. St. Clair's continued financial support and connection to his brother suggest he did not disapprove of this arrangement. Over the course of his travels along the river, St. Clair encountered people from all backgrounds living in all manner of ways, and his worldly view likely fostered a tolerance for his brother's choices. With a reputation as a "ladies' man" who was also very fond of children, it is even possible he cared deeply for his nieces and nephews, enough to intervene and prevent them from being sold away into a life of unbearable servitude.[20]

Later in life, St. Clair was often interviewed about his days as a captain on the river during the golden age of the steamboat. He relished sharing his reminisces about his glory days. The world-famous singer Jenny Lind once traveled aboard his most famous steamboat, the *Magnolia*. Thomasson struck up a friendship with the Swedish meadowlark and thought she might appreciate some of the region's "plantation songs."[21] So, he had the steamboat's band, comprised of Black singers and musicians, perform for her. "There was one likely young boy among them, who had such a voice as you never heard," St. Clair recalled. "I was younger then, by considerable, than I am now, but I could never hear that boy sing . . . without tears coming into my eyes." As one of the musicians kept time with a banjo, the singer also elicited tears from Jenny Lind and inspired her to take to the piano and try and replicate the tune. What was the subject of the song that so deeply moved the captain and the famous soprano? St. Clair recalled, "It was about a yellow girl who had been sold off into slavery from her Louisiana home into Georgia. I always thought the boy made it up himself. I never hear[d] the words or the music before or since." As St. Clair he listened to the song, did he think of his brother's wife Milly?

2

BEING ONCE FREE

Alice Thomasson

Alexander Thomasson's fortunes did not seem to improve significantly after the trial that exposed his debts and his relationship with Milly. He continued to captain vessels on Bayou Lafourche and struggled to make ends meet. For a while, he was master of the *Victress,* a fast-running steamer to Donaldsonville.[1] Because storms, wrecks, explosions, and overall wear and tear wreaked havoc on steamboats, most only lasted seven to nine years before being sold for parts.[2] A steamboat captain benefited from deep pockets, shrewd business sense, and a great deal of luck. Alexander had purchased his latest boat, the *Chalmette,* with his partner Peter Dalferes in 1849. They operated her as a packet steamer from New Orleans to Bayou Lafourche ports, particularly Lockport.[3] On May 14, 1850, the *Chalmette* was pummeled by a destructive storm just one mile from Donaldsonville. The vessel suffered serious damage: both of her chimneys were gone, and her upper works were a complete wreck.[4] Alexander and Dalferes, desperate for the insurance money, then became parties in a lawsuit involving the men who had sold them the vessel and its previous owners. Financial insolvency loomed.[5]

Shaken by the threat of enslavement of his family, Alexander took steps to ensure the safety of his wife and children. The Thomassons traveled together up the Mississippi River to its confluence with the Ohio River at Cairo, Illinois, and, from there, along the Ohio River to Cincinnati.[6]

They would live as free people on free soil. There was a precedent for seeking freedom in Ohio. The Ohio River at Cincinnati served as an important boundary between free and slave states: enslaved people stood on the banks of the Ohio River in Kentucky and looked across to freedom. Ohio became the epicenter of the Underground Railroad. It is estimated that 40 percent of fugitive slaves—approximately forty thousand individuals—crossed the Ohio River to freedom.[7] The Thomassons were among the freedom seekers who sought refuge in Ohio. In fact, the lieutenant governor—and briefly governor—of Louisiana during Reconstruction, P. B. S. Pinchback, son of a free woman of color formerly enslaved by his white father, sought refuge in Cincinnati with his nine siblings when his father's white heirs threatened to reenslave them.[8]

During the Thomassons' time in Cincinnati, the city's population of free people color was the third largest in the nation. It was thus a perfect location for the biracial family that provided Alexander with easy access to the country's main waterways and the steamboat trade.[9] As often was the case when the majority of the family was of mixed race, the census taker marked Alexander Thomasson as a mulatto; there are cases in which white men took on the race of their wife to comply with social norms or to legitimately marry when interracial unions were forbidden. Milly's name was recorded as "Amelia." The couple had four of their children living with them in 1850: Clara, age seventeen, Emma, age fifteen, Alice, age nine, and one-year-old Sarah.[10] Their brother, Alfred, around thirteen years old, was likely working on a steamboat as a cabin boy or in some other menial position, perhaps even on his uncle St. Clair's boat.

Milly Thomasson and her children's claim to freedom was supported by numerous court cases. In 1834, the Louisiana Supreme Court presided over *Louis, f.m.c., vs. Cabarrus*. Previously enslaved in Louisiana, Louis had lived in Ohio for as long as four years. He argued that because Ohio's constitution prohibited slavery, he should be considered free. The Louisiana Supreme Court ruled that the intent of Louis's owner was what determined whether he would be free. It was decided that "the permission given by the master to his slave, to go and labor in the state of Ohio, had the effect to emancipate him."[11] Similarly in *Frank, f.m.c., v. Powell* (1838), the Supreme Court of Louisiana ruled that the man who owned Frank had brought him to Ohio and thus "had submitted himself and the property he brought with him, to the operation of the constitution and laws of that state." Chief Judge Martin explained, "Every man is presumed to have consented to all the necessary legal consequences of his actions. The emancipation of a slave brought into the state of Ohio, is the necessary legal consequences of his removal thither; and his former owner, by whose agency his removal is effected, must have presumed to have consented to that emancipation."[12] Because Alexander Thomasson brought Milly and his children to Ohio with the intention of having them live as free people, they were in fact emancipated. Louisiana Supreme Court judge Edward Simon took it one step further in 1840 in *Thomas v. Generis,* which held that because Thomas had resided on free soil, she was, in fact, free. Simon wrote in his opinion, "Being once free, she could not be again made a slave by removing her to a slave state."[13] This paved the way for the Thomassons to return to Louisiana in the future without the fear of ever again being seized to pay Alexander's debts and enslaved.

Despite the passage of a law in 1846 by the Louisiana state legislature that would deny freedom to slaves who had been brought to free states, the Louisiana Supreme Court initially upheld its previous judgments. It continued to maintain the freedom of people who had gained liberty through transport to free states before 1846.[14] However, with increased hostility toward free people of color and tensions growing over slavery throughout the country, Louisiana's Supreme Court's position changed: it began to reject the notion that an enslaved person who had lived in a free state was thereafter free. The Fugitive Slave Act of 1850, requiring enslaved people in free states to be returned to their owners despite residence in a place where slavery was prohibited, further supported the shift in the Louisiana Supreme Court's stance.

While maintaining a home base in Cincinnati, Alexander continued to ply the waters of Louisiana. He typically captained steamboats coming from Bayou Lafourche into the Mississippi River and then on to New Orleans. He maintained a relationship with his brother and likely visited the *Magnolia* frequently. He may have even seen his brother off on his most auspicious voyage. The *Magnolia* teemed with life that early spring day, and as St. Clair oversaw preparations for departure, he anticipated this trip with great zeal. Jenny Lind, the Swedish nightingale, had just awed the city during her American tour. The world-famous opera singer had enraptured audiences at the St. Charles Theatre. To continue Lind's tour, P. T. Barnum, Lind's manager, arranged passage for her and her followers aboard the *Magnolia*, a vessel known to transport the most distinguished families in the country in luxury and comfort. St. Clair would personally oversee Lind's accommodations on her cross-country voyage, accompany her to the dining room, shield her from adoring fans, and ultimately present to her the glories of Niagara Falls, a vista beloved to him, to which he would return again and again.[15]

Whenever Alexander entered and exited the *Magnolia* on the stage planks connecting it to the shore, he would have met Charles Grice, the boat's eager young clerk, directing freight into the hold. Now in his third season aboard the *Magnolia*, Charles was beginning to come into his own and would eventually be hailed as one of the best steamboat officers on the river. Born in Elizabeth City, North Carolina, a town his ancestors helped found, Charles grew up in a family of shipbuilders. The Grices were masters of trading schooners that transported commodities across the Caribbean and the Chesapeake Bay; they owned boats and enslaved people and ran a profitable enterprise. The advent of the steamboat era brought his father James M. Grice to New Orleans, along with his young family. Despite the chaos, the bustle of passengers, and last-minute communications, Charles would have recognized the captain's brother and taken time to talk with him. His father had also experienced a damaging loss during his time on the river, and Charles sympathized with Alexander's situation.[16]

On a trip downriver from Yazoo City, Captain James M. Grice, Charles's father, had watched in horror as his steamboat the *Ione* caught fire off the banks of St. James Parish. Its cargo of eleven hundred bales of dry cotton and strong winds on the river fueled the fire's rapid spread, which utterly destroyed the boat in fifteen minutes. While the clerk, W. G. Weed, attempted to save the account books and letters, Captain Grice fought to rescue his family. He and his pilot saved his wife Ann and youngest child James. Captain Grice's cousin managed to get five-year-old Alice ashore. The steward, a Black man, saved Charles, age four. Newspaper accounts described the daring rescue in detail, stating that the steward "at the imminent risk of his life plunged into the water with him, and almost reached the shore, when his strength failing him, he was obliged to give up his little charge, but was immediately relieved by the mate of the boat . . . and both were safely landed." The blaze decimated the steamboat: nothing could be saved. The clerk and a fireman were lost, as well as the Black barkeep, a Black chambermaid, the Grice children's nurse, and three passengers. The newspaper made sure to mention that "the captain, crew and passengers return[ed] their most sincere thanks to "Sosthene Roman of Magnolia Plantation, who crossed the river to assist them and offered them the use of his house."[17]

Despite the traumatic experience and horrific loss, Charles's father soon resurrected his steamboat venture. He must have had better insurance and greater funds than Alexander Thomasson. For a time, he was master of the *North Alabama,* the regular packet to Natchez, but he had grander plans.[18] Soon the "long and popularly known . . . navigator of the 'Big Drink'" purchased the steamer *Missouri*. The papers and riverboat men showered the *Missouri* with effusive praise. They considered it "one of the wonders of the age."[19] When it docked at the levee opposite the New Orleans Custom House in 1842, the *Daily Picayune* crowned it "the greatest boat ever on these waters." The reporter encouraged readers to visit it, because he could not provide an adequate description of the *Missouri*'s wonders, other than to write that it was "longer, higher up, deeper, wider, bigger round, measures more, weighs heavier, looks better, and runs faster, than any other craft that ever stuck her nose in the mud about 'these diggings.'"[20] The steamboat era was at its height, and these floating river palaces were not just means of transportation but also were cultural icons. Aboard his father's mammoth boat, visiting the bustling river ports of Vicksburg, Natchez, and New Orleans, Charles experienced a new luxurious age of travel, encountered people from all walks of life, and learned the trade that would provide his living.

This glorious adventure did not last long. Just two years later, James Grice was dead.[21] Charles's mother, Ann, had succumbed to yellow fever in the summer of 1839, one of thirteen hundred people to perish in New Orleans in the epidemic that year.[22] Her obituary noted that "four small children have been deprived by her death of the care of a mother and a fond husband of the companionship of a beloved wife."[23] Charles's youngest sibling, Mary Louise, was just an infant at the time. With his father's passing, Charles and his siblings were orphans and at the mercy of relatives and friends of the family. Though his uncle was technically the children's guardian and his younger siblings were taken in by the family of his father's second wife—a marriage that lasted barely long enough to document—Charles was expected to find a way to survive on his own.[24] His knowledge of the river's twists and turns, gathered over years spent at his father's side, would provide a means. It is likely that he became a cabin boy or hand on one of the boats owned by captains who had respected his father. By 1848, when Charles was fifteen years old, St. Clair Thomasson hired him as clerk aboard the *Magnolia,* a marvelous accomplishment for a young man and a sign of the captain's confidence in his abilities. Once again, Charles traveled up the river, conversing with famous opera stars, laborers, planters, slaves, gamblers, thieves, and families on holiday.

By the mid-1850s, Alexander Thomasson and his family had returned to New Orleans. Alexander probably liked the young clerk and decided to invite him to their home. His wife Milly and daughters Emma, Milly, Alice, and Sarah would certainly love to be regaled with stories of Jenny Lind. One of his daughters would find Charles's affability and charms especially irresistible. No accounts written by Alice are extant, so we need to turn to letters written by contemporaries in similar circumstances to understand her excitement about Charles. Free woman of color Emma Hoggatt, living in New Orleans in 1857 just like Alice, also had a connection to steamboats; her husband and brother were both barbers on board riverboats. Emma described her sister's infatuation with a man who worked on a steamboat: "And as soon as Tene knows that that man's boats in and he don't come to the house," Hoggatt wrote her aunt, "she dresses herself and goes to see him and before she was acquainted with this man a month she went and gave him a daguerratype [sic]." Hoggatt was concerned about her sister's behavior toward a man whose character might prove untrue.[25] Fortunately for Alice, Charles Grice's love for her remained steadfast for more than two decades.

After returning to New Orleans, Alexander became the captain of the *Mary Matilda*, a schooner that made trips across Lake Pontchartrain and to Biloxi, Mississippi.[26] The family lived just across the river from the French Quarter in a neighborhood known as Algiers. Their home was near the Vallette dry docks, a fitting locale for a man who had made a living on the water.[27] Unfortunately they arrived to find increased tensions and restrictions on free people of color. By 1857, Louisiana had prohibited the emancipation of enslaved people: no longer could anyone be freed in the state. State leaders discussed the possible expulsion of free people of color from Louisiana.[28] Many members of that community in New Orleans left the state because of the discrimination and hostility toward them. Some went to Mexico. But the Thomassons had just come home and were reluctant to leave again.

The New Orleans city government by this time was more serious about enforcing the law that required free people of color born or freed outside the city to register with the Mayor's Office. On September 6, 1859, Milly Thomasson and her eldest son Alfred were the first of the family to register. She presented an affidavit signed by her husband and stable keeper William Mish stating that she was free. She told the government official that she had first arrived in Louisiana around 1825 when she was about eight years old. Currently she was employed as a washer and ironer. Despite an exhaustive search through countless records, William Mish's significance has yet to be determined; he may merely have been an acquaintance of the family and a willing witness. Alfred stated that he was around twenty-two years old and, when asked his occupation, replied "steamboating." Clara Thomasson did not register; it's quite likely that she either remained in Ohio or had died. The next four Thomasson siblings registered at the Mayor's Office alongside their mother the following month. They presented a certificate from William Mish and their mother testifying

Photograph of freed formerly enslaved children (*from left,* Rosina Downs, Charles Taylor, and Rebecca Huger) from New Orleans, taken by Charles Paxson in 1864 and used to promote the abolitionist cause up North. The complexions of these children reflect how the people written about in this book might have appeared and underscore race as a social construct. Library of Congress, Prints and Photographs Division, Liljenquist Family Collection.

to their free status. Sisters Emma, Alice, and Sarah Jane then worked as seamstresses. The youngest child, Edward O., was only five years old. The family members were assigned racial descriptors based mostly on phenotype, rather than ancestry. The government official looked at them and determined the proper racial descriptor based on their appearance. All the Thomassons were described as mulattoes, except for Alice.[29]

Recorded as a nineteen-year-old "light mulatresse," Alice stood five feet, three inches high, slightly taller than her older sister Emma. There are no known extant images of Alice, so these physical details are particularly valuable. Yet they do not capture her true essence. At the time, she was a new mother. Her first child, Robert Alfred Grice, had been born less than two months before.[30] She was living as the wife of Charles Grice, a white man, and she was registering as a free woman of color in an official document kept by the city. She could not legally marry the man she loved or legitimize her child, rendering herself and her son vulnerable and without protection under the law. New Orleans society would scorn her and dismiss her as an immoral concubine who had seduced a white man. Like her father and mother, Alice longed for her family to have the same rights as other citizens. More than anything she wanted her relationship with Charles recognized as valid and her children acknowledged as his. It would take a Civil War with thousands of lives lost and a nation on its knees for her dream to be realized.

3

ALL THE SOCIAL QUALITIES OF A GENTLEMAN

Alice Thomasson Grice

Alice would have lined the children up before her and examined them closely that fateful April day in 1871. She wanted to be sure that all shoes were shined, all buttons slipped neatly through holes, and hair sat smoothly and tamed on their heads. The volatile arrival of spring made it difficult to determine the proper dress for them. It was a time of change, of shifting temperatures and skies, when traces of winter's cold could still be felt even as spring's warmth descended. The past winter had been particularly severe; the freezes had decimated the orange crops across the river, and Charles had shivered on the deck of the *Natchez* as it navigated through the river's winds. It was fifty-two degrees when they awoke that morning, but after a few hours the bright sunshine would necessitate the stripping of sweaters and shawls.[1]

It was no small task to bathe, dress, assemble, and inspect the children. Four of them stood before her now, their faces reflecting unique combinations of their mother and father. Three boys and one lone girl. She thought of her other daughter, the missing one: Charlotte Mary Grice. The priest baptized her a few months after her birth in February 1864; when she was seventeen months old, shortly after the end of the Civil War that had cast a shadow across their city and their marriage, the priest officiated at her funeral.[2] The family was headed out to see a different priest now but at the same church it had attended for nearly a decade.

Alice would certainly have known that the loss of an infant was a common occurrence. She lived not far from the cemeteries where wagons brought small caskets and grieving parents every day. Her own sister Emma had no surviving children. Alice knew Emma was on her way to meet them. She shepherded her living children out the door of 91 Gasquet Street, between Claiborne and Robertson, the home she and Charles had shared for more than a decade.[3] The Grice family walked down Gasquet less than three blocks, then turned onto Marais St., and headed down one block more to Tulane Avenue, where St. Joseph Catholic Church's tall front steeple cast a shadow across the street.

Raised by a Creole father, Alice knew that *marais* was the French word for "swamp." The name was appropriate for a street in their neighborhood. A recent addition to the city's landscape, the Tulane-Gravier neighborhood lay far back from the river in what was formerly swamp land. Tracts of old land grants and plantations had been sold, the cypress felled in the woods, and modest shotguns, camelbacks, and cottages began to line the unpaved streets. Far from the elite old French Quarter or the wealth of the increasingly fashionable Uptown area, this was a neighborhood of working people, new arrivals, and faces of every color and ethnicity. It was the perfect location for a woman considered by society to be a quadroon and the white man she lived with as her husband to raise a family without eliciting many questions.

St. Joseph's, a thriving bulwark of the community, had stood on Tulane Avenue opposite Charity Hospital for nearly three decades. The 1844 Gothic edifice was erected for the Irish population in the area and now included a school for boys taught by the Christian Brothers and a school for girls under the direction of the Daughters of Charity.[4] It is likely the Grice children were educated at these institutions. Father Dennis D. Leyden, the young Vincentian priest awaiting them, had arrived in New Orleans a few years after the Civil War. A "gifted" priest, Leyden made "everyone love him, and show[ed] love and attachment for his vocation." A Vincentian leader sent to make a report on the order in the United States deemed

Leyden of "good talents, good education, good appearance." Yet he was a flawed man, possessing a "defect [that] obscures all his good qualities, a penchant for alcohol which exposes him [to danger] and gravely compromises him." Leyden admitted to this weakness and was working to address his alcoholism, no easy feat in a city like New Orleans. He thus seemed the perfect priest for the steamboat men.[5]

The Civil War had interrupted Charles Grice's time on the river. The arrival of the Union Army in the spring of 1862 and its blockading of ports effectively shut down river traffic. In place of steamboats carrying cotton, sugar, and passengers, gunboats appeared on the Mississippi full of soldiers, supplies, and cannons. Thomas P. Leathers, Charles's captain and an ardent Confederate, initially sent his steamboat *Natchez* upriver to the Yazoo River to keep it from falling into Union hands. Nevertheless, the *Natchez* was soon impressed by General P.G.T. Beauregard to serve at White River and Memphis beginning in April 1862. Its bow reinforced by a protruding iron ram, it was used to attack and damage enemy ships. The *Natchez* burned along with the hopes of the Confederacy.[6]

When commercial steamboat traffic on the Mississippi River almost entirely disappeared, Charles Grice was left without a way to earn a living right at the time he had a growing family to support. He decided not to cast his fate with either army. Neither a Union nor a Confederate soldier, he found ways to earn money selling goods and acting as a merchant. In late 1862, he sold hay to the Confederate quartermaster at Port Hudson and received $546.57 from the Confederate government for the "forage."[7] Later in the war, Charles worked in the Opelousas Railroad office.[8] By late 1865, just a few months after the end of the war, Leathers was the captain of the steamboat *Magenta* and sought approval from the U.S. Department of the Gulf to once again move cotton. Charles soon returned to the river with his former captain.[9]

Leathers's new steamboat, the *Magenta*, was only a year old and had cost him a small fortune. Like his old boat, the *Natchez*, it left New Orleans every Saturday evening for Vicksburg and all intermediate landings. Charles's presence on the *Magenta* was a testament to his skill and integrity, because Leathers "employ[ed] none but the most competent men for every department, and they very soon learn[ed] that no neglect of duty, or even the slightest omission on their part [could] escape his observation." Now thirty-two years old and a veteran clerk with seventeen years on the river, Charles was well known in New Orleans, Natchez, and Vicksburg and all the plantation landings and villages in between. He was regularly mentioned in the papers, and his return to the river was heralded with fanfare by the *Daily Picayune,* which considered him "at home again. . . . We very well know there is not an old drayman, white or Black, in New Orleans or at any port between here and Vicksburg who will not rejoice at the announcement that 'Mister Charley' is again at his post, and prepared as formerly to receive just double as many goods in the same given time that any other clerk on the Levee can do, and in all cases do it correctly, and give satisfaction."[10]

Although many were suffering economic losses because of the war, Charles thrived under the leadership of Captain T. P. Leathers, serving as an officer aboard the most famous steamboat of its time and securing himself a position in the middle class. His well-earned success, attributed to his "promptness and correctness" in managing the freight office, gave him "all the social qualities of a gentleman."[11] Even though the *Magenta* was a solid vessel, Leathers apparently never stopped longing for his lost *Natchez;* he was determined to have another, bigger, better, and grander steamboat than before. In the spring of 1868, Charles took command of the *Magenta* while Leathers traveled to commission and oversee the construction of the new *Natchez.*[12] Charles must certainly have enjoyed the addition of "captain" to his name.

When it sailed into New Orleans, the new *Natchez* was deemed "the most easy, graceful, and perfect model" of steamboat "ever seen." This "rich, sumptuous" steamer had fifty-six staterooms for gentlemen and ladies, as well as four bridal chambers; they were furnished with lace and damask curtains, red velvet carpet, and mahogany furniture. Guests dined on lavish fare with tables laid out with silver and china. Eight chandeliers illuminated the main cabin. The mammoth texas deck—the uppermost desk—contained four departments: the captain's quarters with a parlor and two bedrooms; the officers' quarters where Charles Grice slept, with a hall and eight rooms; a cabin boy's department with a hall and ten rooms; and a "new feature in steamboat nomenclature," visible evidence of the changes wrought by the war, a "Freedmen's Bureau" quarters for people of color. This addition consisted of a hall and twelve rooms, including two bridal chambers. The "bureau" was "altogether separate and distinct from the main cabin," and meals were served there to ensure that white guests would not share a table with Black travelers.[13] Had Alice and the Grice children ever accompanied Charles on one of his voyages, what space would they have occupied? Would they have adhered to societal dictates, occupying the "Freedmen's" department, or would they have attempted to occupy one of the ostentatious staterooms?

As the *Natchez* was being built, the Grice family became property holders. Given Charles's success and income, he would seem to be the one to purchase a home for the family. Yet it was through Alice's efforts that a lot of land came into their possession. On January 7, 1867, William O'Brien sold Alice a lot of land fronting Banks Street, bounded by Palmyra, Tonti, and Miro Streets, for $600. She paid O'Brien $200 in cash at the time of the sale. He granted her a mortgage for the remaining $400, which would be paid in a year's time with 6 percent interest. If the mortgage was not paid in full, the interest rate would rise to 8 percent.[14]

How Alice obtained the money for this purchase remains a mystery. Perhaps Charles provided the funds. Yet if that were the case, why was the sale made in her name and not his? Did Charles want to ensure that if anything happened to him the property would remain in Alice's hands, even though she and the children were technically not allowed to inherit? Or Alice could have gotten the funds from her father, provided by his activities in manipulating funds.

Alexander Thomasson's last years were spent working as a barkeep, the career path he initially rejected thirty years before. He lived with Milly, whom he considered his wife, and their children just across the river from New Orleans in Algiers, where he died on June 13, 1866. The *Daily Picayune* ran a one-sentence obituary for him, referring to him as "Capt. Alex. Thomasson" and attributing his death to pneumonia.[15] Alice herself reported his death; her signature graces the bottom of his death certificate.[16]

His financial struggles would have made filing for a succession unnecessary, because all his money was probably owed to creditors. The fact that he was not legally married and that his "natural" children's illegitimacy would bar them from inheriting would also have complicated matters. If he had any money or property at all at the time of his death, he would have had to evade creditors and avoid a succession that would have entitled his siblings but not his wife and children to his possessions. It is entirely possible that knowing he was ill and near death, Thomasson gave his daughter Alice $200. The timing and circumstances indicate that this is indeed what happened. Thomasson died in June; less than seven months later Alice appeared before a notary public with the cash on hand to verify a sale on the Banks Street lot.

The seemingly mundane notarized bill of sale, yellowed and crackling with age and dry legalese, holds two significant clues about Charles and Alice. Even though they were not legally married, it refers to Alice as the "wife of Charles Grice." Charles was even present at the settlement, signing to acknowledge that the property was his wife's and not part of a shared community between them. Technically this signed legal document, even though it was notarized and witnessed, was invalid because the Grices were not legally married. Yet the fact that they would refer to themselves as husband and wife even in a legal transaction indicates their depth of feeling and commitment. Alice was not just Charles's mistress, to be tossed aside when she no longer pleased him. Their children were not to go unacknowledged; Charles did not view them as his racial, social, or economic inferiors. The Grices were a family, whether the law allowed them to be one or not.

The signatures that appear at the end of the document, in addition to Charles's, are another telling aspect of the sale. William O'Brien's wife, Mary Dunn, had to approve the sale and renounce her stake in the property, so she too was present in the notary's office. At the end of the transaction, as O'Brien and then Charles took up their pens and scrawled their names across the page, Mary informed the notary that she was unable to write and would have to witness with her "ordinary mark." Mary, a white woman, formed an X on the paper and then handed the pen to Alice, a former slave. Alice confidently and legibly applied her signature to the document, illustrating that, in nineteenth-century New Orleans, race did not dictate literacy. A formerly enslaved Creole woman of mixed race, daughter of a slave and a steamboat captain, might be able to read and write, while a white Irish immigrant, lacking an education, was incapable of even spelling her name.

The Banks Street lot, only a few blocks away from their Gasquet Street home, kept the Grices in the Tulane-Gravier neighborhood. Construction of the Banks Street home would take time to complete, and meanwhile they continued to occupy their rented house on Gasquet, where the census taker found them in 1870. Alice spent her days keeping house and raising her children, and Charles's position as a river clerk was noted. Once again, there was difficulty in classifying the Grices. The available racial options—white, Black, or mulatto—did not cover the nuanced caste system left over from New Orleans's colonial era. The census taker listed Alice as mulatto and Charles as white. He deemed the eldest son Robert white as well, perhaps because of his complexion. Yet the three youngest Grice children he determined to be mulattoes like their mother. The presence of other residents in the household further emphasizes the Grices' improved circumstances: Mary Pierre and Martha Fuller, age fifteen and twelve, respectively, worked as Black domestic servants for the Grices. Alice did not keep house alone: she had help with the cooking, cleaning, washing, and scrubbing.[17] If Charles Grice had "all the social qualities of a gentleman," then Alice had acquired the status of a lady—at least in every way but the eyes of the law. This was about to change.

When Alice, Charles, and their four children walked into St. Joseph Catholic Church that spring day in 1871, Father Leyden met them and escorted them up the aisle. Alice and Charles knelt at the altar, while their children sat in the pews with their Aunt Emma and watched as their parents were both sacramentally and legally bound to each other. After the exchange of vows, Father Leyden documented the marriage in the church's sacramental record book. He then wrote the names of the children in Latin, noting that they were now legitimized. The surviving Grice children born before their parents' legal marriage were Robert Alfred, age eleven;

Bertha Louisa, age nine; Charles Francis, age four; and Joseph Augustus, age two.[18] Though the Civil War and reconstruction of the South that followed brought tremendous change—enslaved people were free, could own property, and learn to read and write; Black men could vote; former slaves could legitimize marriages entered into during slavery; and people of color could now legally marry—one of the last vestiges of the old social hierarchy remained firmly entrenched. Miscegenation, the intermarrying of whites and Blacks, remained illegal. Charles and Alice must have rejoiced when the laws were finally rewritten, and the Louisiana Civil Code of 1870 became the governing force in the land, no longer barring interracial marriage.[19] Within a year of its passage, the Grices legalized their union and were finally recognized as the family they had always truly been.

Charles spent the early 1870s aboard the *Natchez*, the "old friend" of the riverfront, heralded as "'king' of the freight department" by the newspapers.[20] During the summer, the *Natchez* and Captain Leathers stayed in port for repairs and a rest. But the Vicksburg and *Natchez* river traffic, even in the off-season, still needed to go on, so Charles became "Captain Grice" and commanded a variety of other steamers.[21] Another daughter joined the Grice family in February 1873, the year a serious economic depression rocked the nation. Alice was baptized at St. Joseph's the following month, with her older siblings Robert and Bertha standing as godparents.[22] The Grices seemed a growing, devoted family and Charles an able and successful worker, yet all was not well. He had to take a hiatus from the *Natchez* in August 1874. He went fishing for several weeks to "restore his shattered nerves."[23] The arrival of twin daughters two and a half years later possibly increased his stress.

The Grices christened their three daughters born in the 1870s with ornate, whimsical, even saintly names. Alice, named for her mother, was entered into the baptismal register as Alice Olivia Comadina Grice. The twin girls born on March 24, 1876, were christened Angela Clotilda Bernadetta Grice and Emma Maude Clotaire Grice.[24] Emma died on August 1 of that same year at only four months old.[25] Two years later Alice delivered James Oscar Grice. Baptized less than a month after his birth, it appears he was given his middle name in honor of his godfather Oscar Dubuclet.[26]

Dubuclet, only seventeen at the time, was on break from the College of the Holy Cross in Worcester, Massachusetts. His father Antoine, a free man of color prior to the war, had owned a large plantation and many slaves in Iberville Parish. He was the wealthiest Black property owner in the South. During Reconstruction, he was elected state treasurer, an office he held for ten years. The Dubuclets were neighbors of the Grices; they lived just a few houses away on Gasquet Street.[27] Though the Grices often made choices that cloaked their mixed racial ancestry, their selection of Dubuclet as James's godfather demonstrated they still maintained a connection to people of color and did not yet isolate themselves from that community.

The Grices' financial and health struggles overwhelmed them by 1879. The Vicksburg newspaper reported in January of that year that Charles, "identified with the Vicksburg and New Orleans trade for years," had quit the *Natchez*.[28] He had worked with Captain Leathers for nearly thirty years and served on three different steamboats christened *Natchez*. For three decades, Charles traveled up and down that great river. Now he planned to run a cotton yard in New Orleans, keeping him at home. He could no longer handle the demands of constant travel and the grueling work on the riverboat. In fact, the *Daily Picayune* made his situation very clear: "He was compelled to give up his position on account of physical infirmities."[29]

Yet Charles did not seem entirely prepared to walk away from his career on the river. A month and a half later, the same newspaper that reported his retirement to a cotton yard informed readers that Charles was now clerk of the *Lucy E. Gastrell* and that "he [was] a good one."[30] In fact, the *Picayune* would later clarify that Charles was captain of that steamer, the weekly packet to Grand Gulf.[31] By May, Captain Gastrell met "Captain Charley Grice" in Natchez to make arrangements for his steamer the *City of Augusta* to enter the New Orleans and Vicksburg trade and to be commanded by Grice.[32] However, this last endeavor did not come to pass. Charles ended his career as a steamboat captain commanding the *Lucy E. Gastrell* in the Davis Bend trade.

The prosperity the Grices had enjoyed ended with Charles's departure from the river. Even young Charles, only thirteen years old, then had to contribute to the family's income. He left school and worked as a tobacco salesman.³³ Alice sold the Banks Street lot and home to New Orleans Credit Foncier Association for $1,060.25, probably because the Grices needed to settle some debts and they had no ready cash. Only a few days after the New Orleans Credit Foncier Association acquired ownership of the property, Alice bought it back from them. On September 2, 1879, she officially reacquired the Banks Street home for $1,237.25. She put down only $5 in cash in the transaction and endorsed three promissory notes of $410.75 each, payable in one, two, and three years at an annual interest rate of 8 percent. This gave the Grices access to the equity they had built in the property to assist with their financial troubles but left them with a large mortgage and virtually nothing invested in their home.³⁴

In addition to Charles's struggles, his forced retirement, and the financial problems plaguing the family, Alice's health began to deteriorate. She developed serious respiratory issues and was pregnant yet again, this time with her last child. Giving birth to ten children over twenty years certainly did not help her overall condition. In September 1880, Effie, the Grice's youngest child, became the last addition to the Banks Street home.³⁵

Alice died at home on Banks Street on April 5, 1883. Only forty-two years old and with her youngest child just two, she left the world on a warm, wet spring day. Clouds hovered over the city. Business on the riverfront was stagnant, and races at the fairgrounds were postponed.³⁶ It was as if the gloom that settled over the Grice household at Alice's passing pervaded all of New Orleans. Charles, perhaps too distraught to perform the duty himself, let his adult son Robert report her death. He appeared before the recorder with a certificate from Dr. E. D. Beach testifying that Alice died of tuberculosis. Robert then did something that would shift the course of his life and that of his siblings. Whether his decision had been a calculated one, a plan the Grices had long hoped to put into place, or a spontaneous declaration on his part remains a mystery. He told the recorder that his mother Alice was white and a native of France. This information was recorded on her official death certificate.³⁷

Passing as white was not unknown to the Grices. Alice's sister Emma had appeared in census records as white since 1860. She lived with a white man, whom she apparently considered her husband, for more than forty years. Like her father and brother-in-law, William Crockett had a career on the river; his work on steamboats was likely the way the couple met.[38] Margaret Tregre Grossinger, a close neighbor, friend, and Creole quadroon like Alice, also identified as white.[39] A change in racial identity seems to be something Alice and Charles had considered for herself and the children.

The children's birth certificates indicate an evolving racial identity over a span of nearly two decades. When Robert's birth was recorded, he was called "Robert Alfred Grice Thomasson" and was referred to as a "natural child," born of parents who were not legitimately married. His race was unequivocally "colored."[40] Three years later, Bertha was issued a "colored" birth certificate, though her surname was Grice, not Thomasson.[41] Although Charles was born in 1866, the Grices waited another seven years to officially report it; at the time they also registered the births of Joseph (1868) and Alice (1873). No race was recorded for them. They even had a new certificate issued for Bertha that omitted her race. When the twins were born, their race was also left blank.[42] The year they were born marked the end of Reconstruction in Louisiana. Former Confederates and white supremacists quickly regained power, and race became the central issue dominating politics, economics, and social life. Ambiguous birth certificates stopped being issued. A cursory examination of births recorded in Orleans Parish beginning in the late 1870s and 1880s reveals only W's and C's, with no omissions. Perhaps this was why Alice and Charles chose not to register James or Effie's births. There would be no paper trail, no legal documents that bound them to their one-eighth African heritage or even hinted at it.

Charles's death a year after Alice's was sudden, though his decline in health was not. His family and friends knew he had been ailing for some years and yet expected him to continue on in that way, not anticipating an abrupt loss. The children all gathered at the Banks Street house, so many of them and spanning so many years they seemed to make up two generations of Grices instead of one. Robert, now twenty-five and working as a tinsmith, had lived for a time away from home but was in residence at the time of his father's death. Bertha, age twenty-two, a seamstress, was being courted by a young man whom she would eventually marry. At eighteen, Charles had been out of school and working for several years. Sixteen-year-old Joseph managed to remain in school longer, though he would soon become a waiter and later a celebrated barkeep. The younger children—Alice, Clothilde, James, and Effie—ranged in age from eleven to four.[43]

The Grice children, all eight of them, welcomed the guests as they arrived, the open door letting in the waning light of a late autumn afternoon. It was 3:30 p.m. on November 17, 1884, an average Monday when most of them would otherwise be at work or at school. At 9:00 p.m. the night before, their father had been alive. By 9:15 he was dead, and, according to the custom of the time, less than twenty-four hours later they were holding his funeral. Dr. E. D. Beach, the family physician, noted the cause of death as "serous apoplexy." Charles had suffered a stroke or cerebral hemorrhage. That he had been at home at the time of his death and not on a riverboat was a testament to the ill health he had experienced for many years.[44]

When their father died, the children were still feeling the loss of their mother in their home. Now with Charles gone, the rooms felt empty, even as a crowd gathered to pay their respects. After the funeral service in the residence, they crossed Canal Street, headed for St. Louis Cemetery No. 2 to inter Charles in the same vault occupied by the bodies of their dead baby sister Emma and mother. The North Carolina native received a proper New Orleans above-ground burial in a Catholic cemetery that held the tombs of pirates, nuns, soldiers, tradesmen, voodoo practitioners, enslaved and free, of all shades of color.[45]

The five oldest Grice siblings wrestled with how to take care of their younger brother and sisters. Though he had a job, Robert was a young bachelor, lacking the funds and ability to care for five children. Bertha could not support an entire family on her seamstress salary, and she would soon marry and have her own children. Charles and Joseph, adolescent boys capable of work, were incapable of raising small children. Fortunately, kind neighbors intervened and offered to take in Alice, age eleven; Clothilde, age eight; James, age six, and Effie, age four. Charles and Margaret Grossinger lived on Gasquet Street, just two blocks up and a block over from the Grices. They knew them not only as friends and neighbors but also as fellow parishioners at St. Joseph Catholic Church. The Grossingers, a childless couple, with a background similar to that of the Grices, welcomed the children into their modest four-room home. Grossinger, a Hungarian immigrant and store clerk, had been in a relationship for decades with a Creole quadroon woman now identifying as white, with a past very similar to that of the children's mother. Margaret (formerly Marguerite) and Charles Grossinger would become the only parents little Effie would remember.

4

A COMPLEXION LIKE ALABASTER

Marguerite Tregre

When Marguerite was five years old, she stood on the gallery of the plantation home in which she was enslaved and looked out on a disaster: the steamboat *Meteor* was burning in the Mississippi River. A fire had broken out in the lower deck, and soon the entire boat was shrouded in flames. The boat went up quickly because it was carrying 165 bales of cotton to be sold in New Orleans. Soon people began leaping into the water to escape the vessel that was being devoured by flames. The Duparcs and the Locouls, the plantation owners, rushed out to the steamboat landing, along with their enslaved laborers. Newspaper accounts stated that before the boat reached the shore, the bank was lined with the resident family, enslaved domestic servants, and others from the immediate neighborhood, all anxious to render assistance. Thanks to the diligence of the crew, nearly all the passengers and crew survived. The attitude of the white passengers on disembarking on the levee was that of profound relief. As the newspaper later put it, the "only persons lost" were a free man of color, an enslaved pantry man, and an enslaved cook. Meanwhile the Duparcs and Locouls took the passengers from the abandoned steamboat into their home. A witness later said that crew and passengers both felt that "their solicitude for our safety whilst in peril was only equaled by their kind and hospitable treatment after we landed, and which was extended with an ease, grace, and spirit of kindness characteristic of the noble and generous hearted." Marguerite observed her mother Armantine and the other enslaved domestics scrambling to meet the needs of the traumatized people, taking orders from their masters and mistresses as to how best to assist them.[1]

Marguerite would have taken all this in. It would certainly have been a sensational occurrence on a rural plantation in the nineteenth century, where life was much slower than in the city. What might Marguerite have learned from this? That there was a possibility of leaving the plantation. There were steamboats up and down the river full of passengers headed south to New Orleans and north all the way up into the free states. She would have been struck by the mobility possessed by so many free people that was potentially available for enslaved people who were willing to risk everything to seek freedom. Yet she would also see that leaving the plantation could be dangerous, even deadly. The people who died in the steamboat accident were free people of color and enslaved people, people like her. No one seemed overly concerned about their loss. It's likely that the profit lost in cotton and the Alexandria mail that had gone down in the Mississippi's muddy waters were lamented far more than the loss of people of color. She would grow up dreaming of escape from the plantation and yet filled with trepidation of the unknown. The jeopardy inherent in the outside world would become particularly evident to her when she later became foster mother to children whose parents came from the steamboating tradition. In fact, their father's harrowing rescue from the fire on the steamboat *Ione* had occurred just across the river from the Duparc & Locoul Plantation, eight years before she was born. The Grices remembered fondly Sosthene Roman, who owned Magnolia Plantation, adjacent to the Duparc & Locoul Plantation, for his assistance and for opening his house to them during the tragedy.

Marguerite would never experience biological motherhood, but by taking in the Grice children, she finally realized the maternal role so crucial to a woman's identity in the society of her time. The Grices and Grossingers were a blended family based on bonds forged in friendship and in emotional and physical needs. Marguerite would have easily understood these relationships because her own family background was unconventional. The Grice children had experienced the loss of both parents. Marguerite had in essence a nonexistent father, and her own mother embodied the trauma that came with the wrenching apart of mother and child. Marguerite's story and her mothering of the Grice children cannot be understood without first uncovering the life of her mother Armantine, enslaved on the Duparc & Locoul Plantation in St. James Parish. Armantine's origins link her experiences to those of her own daughter, as well as to those of Alice Thomasson Grice.

In 1836, Flagy Duparc, then a forty-four-year-old married man, attended the auction of the estate of Judge Joseph Fabre, a St. James Parish planter whose death had left his widow with debts to settle. Duparc purchased Armantine, an eleven-year-old Creole mulatresse, just old enough to be sold away legally from her mother. Duparc paid $960 for her, making her the most expensive female slave ever bought by the Duparcs and Locouls; she cost them more than skilled seamstresses, cooks, and housemaids in their prime childbearing years.[2] Her complexion and price indicate that she was sold as a "fancy girl," intended for a life of sexual exploitation. The daughter of white Creole planter Pujol Perret, Armantine was thus the half-sister of Amélie Perret, Judge Fabre's widow. This means that the widow Fabre not only sent her half-sister to be auctioned off but watched as she was sold to a man intent on abusing her.[3]

Armantine lived as an enslaved house servant in the plantation's Big House close to Duparc and alongside his extended family, including his wife, brother, sister-in-law, sister, brother-in-law, and their children. In 1845, when she was twenty years old, she gave birth to Marguerite.[4] Marguerite's father was Séverin Tregre, the plantation's overseer. Within a year, he married Celina Tassin and began what Louisiana law would consider a legitimate family.[5] Tregre, a seemingly devout Catholic with a large family that had lived in Louisiana for generations, spent most of his time in the field, overseeing the enslaved workers as they planted, tended to, and then harvested the sugarcane crop. The plantation was a large one, with 138 enslaved individuals owned by the Duparc Brothers & Locoul Company. In addition to these fieldworkers for the sugarcane enterprise, Guil-

Laura Plantation, formerly known as the Duparc & Locoul Plantation, birthplace of Marguerite Tregre Grossinger. Photograph copyright © ImagoDens | Dreams time.com.

laume Duparc, his mother, and siblings also held in private possession their own enslaved domestics. Guillaume Duparc and his wife Marcelite had thirteen enslaved domestics, including a laundress, housemaids, a valet, a coachman, and Armantine and Marguerite. Séverin Tregre, Marguerite's father, enslaved twelve people. In 1850, when Marguerite was five years old, 190 individuals were held in the bonds of slavery on the Duparc & Locoul Plantation.[6]

Marguerite's first language was French, the same language spoken by the people who enslaved her, as well as by her mother and other enslaved Creoles on the property. Growing up in the Big House, she knew her father's identity, and she was very aware of her many white half-siblings who lived in the overseer's house on the property. Unlike the many enslaved children who were raised in cabins shared with both their mother and father, as well as siblings, Marguerite came of age surrounded by an elite white family who simultaneously showed her special attention and favors while also holding total control over her life. She could be praised one moment and violently punished the next; her mother Armantine would have no say in the matter.

Thus, it was Armantine's job to teach Marguerite how to survive. Marguerite's proximity to the plantation owners meant that her every move was scrutinized. She had to always anticipate the needs of the family that owned her. She had to be both subservient and eager. Her tone of voice mattered. She needed to respond quickly but not be so speedy as to startle anyone. She had to appear neat, clean, and well dressed but by no means seem overly so. And she had to be willing to allow her body to be used. It was the way of things on the plantation. In these ways she was prepared for the life of a "fancy girl," just like her mother and grandmother had been before her.

Armantine would have known what awaited her daughter but was powerless to do anything about it. While observing a Virginia slave auction, journalist James Redpath witnessed a heart-wrenching scene that could easily describe how Armantine must have felt about Marguerite: "The poor black mother—with her nearly white babe—with anxiety of an uncertain future among brutal men before her—and the young girl, too, now so innocent, but predestined by the nature of slavery to a life of . . . involuntary prostitution."[7] For that was the kind of slavery to which Marguerite was bound: she would be forced to suffer sexual coercion and rape. Historian Edward Baptist summed up the situation faced by Marguerite and so many other women held in slavery in the American South when he wrote, "Systematic rape and sexual abuse of slave women were part of the normal practice of the men who ran the firm [slave traders]—and the normal practice of many of their planter customers as well." Slavery, rape, and commerce were all linked, embodying the society that wealthy slave owners had created.[8] The phenotypes of mulatto, quadroon, and octoroon assigned to Armantine, Marguerite, and later Alice and her children were visible evidence of the long history of rape and sexual exploitation that were accepted parts of slavery and southern life.

Marguerite and her mother Armantine were women, as historian Emily Owens so accurately phrased it, for whom "enslavement was defined by sexual service." According to historian Walter Johnson, the term "fancy girl," which was used quite commonly, originated with the concept of fancying or desiring something or someone. These young women were typically of mixed race and brought in a much higher price at auction than even enslaved male artisans like blacksmiths and coopers.[9] Slave trader Isaac Franklin of New Orleans routinely referred to "fancy girls" in his correspondence and often mentioned sexual assault. Free woman of color Sarah Parker Redmond on her lecture tour spoke openly about their fate: "They are sold to be the concubines for white Americans. They are not sold for plantation slaves."[10] In his memoir *Twelve Years a Slave,* Solomon Northup saw firsthand how slave traders would take light-colored enslaved girls and groom them to be sexually exploited. "There were heaps and piles of money to be made of her, he [the trader] said, when she was a few years older," Northup recalled. "She was a beauty—a picture—a doll."[11] Many people would go on to point out that these "fancy girls"—women of European and African descent—held appeal for white planters because of their skin color's proximity to whiteness. The American caste system met with the Creole idea of racial gradations to create a hideous objectification and commodification of mixed-race women for horrific sexual abuse.

Enslaved women were routinely subjected to rape and sexual assault. Considered property under the law, they did not possess the right of consent. White men could and did use them without repercussions. Haller Nutt, a resident of Natchez who owned several plantations including some in Louisiana, enslaved eight hundred people. He complained of overseers raping the women he enslaved; apparently, he considered that a benefit for which he alone qualified. When Isaac Throgmorton was asked about his observations of slavery, he spoke of deplorable conditions on Nutt's plantations: "Mr. Haller Nutt, who lived in Louisiana, was very cruel indeed, & one man on his place was tied up by the thumbs, and whipped awful; the next morning he was a dead man." Why had the man been subjected to this torture? After Nutt raped his wife, the enslaved man expressed his anger, which Nutt believed was "saucy" behavior.[12] During the Civil War, Rufus Kinsley was stationed in Louisiana and witnessed the accepted culture of rape against women of color on plantations. "To-day . . . made the acquaintance of a man . . . who, while living with his wife . . . raised three daughters in less than as many years, by one of his slaves, a quadroon girl," Kinsley wrote in his diary. "About four years ago the quadroon girl was sold, her three daughters, as white as three Yankee girls, remaining with their father, who has since, though the youngest girl is now fifteen only, received an heir by each of them. A little while before our fleet came up the river, two of these heirs, by his own daughters, were sold."[13] Another Union soldier, Lawrence van Alstyne, had a similar experience during his time in Louisiana. He encountered an enslaved woman of mixed race attempting to flee to the North. Her husband had been hanged by the Confederate Army. Van Alstyne saw a picture of him and described him as being "as white as I am . . . the son of his master." The woman's father had been a judge who was also in the "rebel army." He noted that the woman "hopes to reach New York, and I wished I could land here there that minute. If she was dressed as well, and if she was educated, she would pass muster with any I have seen that go by that name."[14] Julia Woodrich, born into slavery on a plantation near Thibodaux, spoke candidly about rape in the slave quarters: "I 'member how my massa use to would come an' get my sister, make her take a bath an' comb her hair an' take her down in the quarter all night—den have de nerve to come aroun' de nex' day an' ax her how she feel. . . . Dats de reason dare is so many mulatto n——r chillins now."[15]

DNA analysis has confirmed a legacy of rape against enslaved women of African descent. Even though most Africans forcibly transported to the United States were male, DNA results show that enslaved African women "contributed to gene pools at a higher rate," about 1.5 to 2 times more than African men. Steven Micheletti and Joanna Mountain, authors of the study published in the *American Journal of Human Genetics,* wrote, "The biases in the gene pool toward enslaved African women and European men signal generations of rape and sexual exploitation against enslaved women at the hands of White owners." Emily Owens underscores this data, noting of women like Armantine and Marguerite, "Their stories make visible the ways that sexual violence was not primarily spectacular, but an everyday occurrence; and that the slave society ritualized, invited, and normalized violent sex against Black women in the language of their own desires."[16] It is important to stress that, although consensual relationships like those of the Thomassons and the Grices did exist, the experiences of Armantine and Marguerite represented the norm. Most interracial sex was, in fact, rape.

Marguerite likely witnessed scenes of extreme brutality that left her with trauma that would burden her for the rest of her life. The Duparcs and Locouls took hot iron brands and applied these to the flesh of enslaved people who ran away from the plantation, just as they would do with cattle. Slaves were forced into the stocks or whipped for transgressions. Not only field hands and laborers but also domestics and skilled artisans experienced this violence. A year before Marguerite's birth, Austin Burgess, a cooper sold south through the interstate slave trade, "absconded" from the plantation. His position as a cooper was an important one; in addition to making barrels, he would have crafted the hogsheads in which the sugar was stored and transported. The Duparcs and Locouls had paid a high price for him and advertised in the newspapers for his return.[17] Though no record remains of what occurred when Burgess was captured and forcibly returned to the plantation, it is likely that he was branded, placed in the stocks, or brutally whipped as punishment for having run away.

Betsey, a laundress and ironer also capable of cooking and sewing, was sold four times in five years. In fact, she was eventually sold for a reduced price, indicating that white enslavers might have considered her rebellious or defiant.[18] One month after arriving at the plantation, she ran away, presumably back to New Orleans. Raymond Locoul placed a runaway slave advertisement in the newspaper, offering a $10 reward.[19] Ultimately Raymond sold Betsy to his mother-in-law Nanette Duparc, who considered her only "fit for the field."[20] Betsy was forced to toil in the cane fields, subject to backbreaking labor and poor living conditions. There was also the constant threat of sale. Louis Duparc's wife sold his two "fancy girls" after his death in 1852.[21] Marguerite's only recognized biological family member was her mother, and she would have been terrified of being separated from her.

Nowhere on this plantation nor, in fact on any plantation in Louisiana, could Marguerite fit in or at least feel a sense of belonging. Her long, straight black hair framed a white complexion. She wore fine dresses; ate nutritious, well-prepared food; slept in conditions far from primitive; and perhaps was even semi-literate. She even had the hope of achieving freedom, because Flagy Duparc's will bequeathed Armantine and Marguerite to his sister Elisabeth, with instructions to free them.[22] Though he later altered the will, the fact that Duparc considered emancipating them was significant: Marguerite and Armantine were the only two enslaved people on the plantation for whom freedom was ever considered. The capture of New Orleans by the Union Army early in the war and the arrival of federal troops on the plantation abruptly ended her and her mother's enslavement on the plantation.

War came to the Duparc & Locoul plantation with the arrival of the Second Louisiana Native Guard, a newly formed regiment of the Union Army made up of free men of color and runaway slaves. It was early November 1862, the height of grinding season, and the enslaved laborers out in the field harvesting sugarcane stopped work at the sight of the soldiers. Colonel Nathan Daniels, the head of the regiment, and his second-in-command, Major Francis Dumas, rode up to the Big House in a buggy. They were led up the stairs to the gallery, where they met owner Flagy Duparc. After having drinks and dinner with Duparc, they camped for the night. The next morning Colonel Daniels made it clear he wanted one enslaved person to accompany him back to his headquarters: Marguerite, a seventeen-year-old quadroon girl whom he had seen the night before in the house.[23]

Colonel Daniels was a thirty-year-old widower from New York and an ardent abolitionist. Despite his progressive ideals, when Daniels first caught sight of Marguerite, his thoughts were not very different from those of Flagy Duparc when he had seen her mother put up for auction decades before. Daniels wrote in his diary that Marguerite "came to me and wished me to take her into a country of Freedom & I did so."[24] Yet Louis Smith, Duparc's driver, testified otherwise under oath. According to Smith, as Daniels and his men prepared to move to the Becnel Plantation, Daniels told Smith he would give him $20 if he brought Marguerite to him at the encampment. Accompanying Marguerite was Martha, an enslaved laundress on the plantation. Marguerite stayed in Colonel Dan-

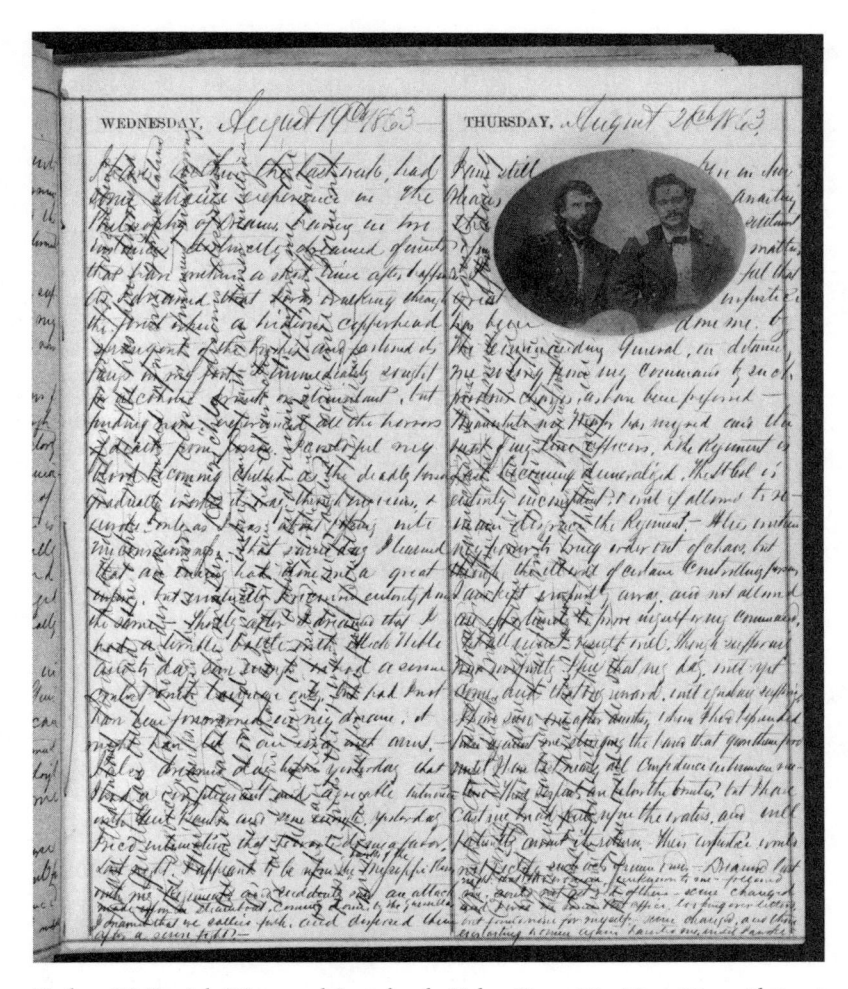

Nathan W. Daniels Diary and Scrapbook, Vol. 1, Dec. 1861–May 1864, with inset photo of Colonel Nathan W. Daniels and Major Francis Dumas. Library of Congress, Manuscript Division.

iels's room, while Martha occupied Major Dumas's quarters. For roughly three months—from November 1862 until January 1863—Colonel Daniels served as provost marshal for St. John the Baptist and St. James Parishes. When the Second Native Guard was sent to Ship Island (off the coast of Mississippi), essentially a form of military exile ordered by General Nathaniel Banks, the new commander of the Department of the Gulf, Daniels left Marguerite in New Orleans. But she would not remain there for long.[25]

In early April 1863, Major Dumas informed Daniels that Marguerite was determined to visit him on Ship Island. "God only knows what could have possessed her to come here now," Daniels wrote. "She is much better off in the city and will have to immediately return." But she obtained a pass to travel from Colonel Chandler, and, after a thirteen-hour boat ride on the schooner *Eliza Ann,* Marguerite arrived in camp. In his diary, Daniels made the nature of his relationship with Marguerite very clear: I "have taken her into my domicile, and established a family." Rather than ordering that she immediately return to the city, as he had claimed he would, Marguerite remained with him on the island for two weeks. During that time, Daniels began to plan for her future. When old friends arrived on a ship from Philadelphia, Daniels wrote that their visit provided "an excellent opportunity to send Margaret to the north to some good school where she can make something of the Refinement and ability that nature hath so bountifully blessed her with." He had her photograph taken, presumably so he could have a memento of her after she was sent to the North "for the next few years."[26]

The evening of her departure, Daniels recorded the story of Marguerite's life, deeming "her history . . . a strange one." He referred to her as "belonging body and soul to an old wealthy French planter," namely Flagy Duparc. "I found her a charming, beautiful Créole woman, with not enough dark blood in her veins to bust their surface," he wrote. She had "long beautiful black hair, rosy cheeks, a complexion like alabaster." He deemed her "refined and intelligent. . . . Gladly did she welcome the Yankees coming although the pet of the southern household & the companion of the master & family." Daniels continued. "She was a lady and free in every thing but her liberty . . . she is now attached to me as her preserver from a life of infamy and shame—as she was intended for by her unfeeling & devilish master." In her work on sexual violence and enslaved women in New Orleans, Emily Owens mentioned Solomon Northup's encounter with an enslaved girl destined for the sex trade. Owens wrote that, in the illustration of the child included in the 1853 publication of *Twelve Years a*

Slave, the "illumination of her bright white skin's contrast to that of her mother calls attention to her body as the inevitable and frequent result of white men's violent sexual contact with enslaved women, which in turn marked those children as always already blighted by sexual violence and thus also already available for further sexual violence." The same could be said for Daniels's description of Marguerite.[27]

Although the Union Army brought Marguerite a degree of freedom, allowing her to leave the plantation where she had been confined and so escape her abuser, she immediately attached herself to another man with questionable intentions who did not hesitate to sexually exploit her. Despite his supposedly enlightened views on matters of race, Daniels did not consider marrying her, and though he deemed himself her "preserver from a life of infamy and shame," he happily began a sexual relationship with her outside marriage, an arrangement that would bring shame and ruin to any nineteenth-century American woman. In fact, in many ways Marguerite seemed to be merely exchanging one master for another. Yet it would be wrong to discount Marguerite's agency in her own life; she knew the value that men placed on sex, she knew she wanted to escape the bonds of the plantation, and perhaps she saw in Daniels an easy way out. It is impossible to know whether she considered their relationship a love affair, a means to an end, or another example of her victimization.

Less than a week after sending Marguerite back to New Orleans, Daniels arrived in the city and broke things off with her, leaving her in rooms on Rampart Street. "Must Divest myself of that encumbrance," he confided to his diary. "There is danger in her connection—and she must be content with what I have already done for her—I can do no more."[28] Daniels's explanation is ambiguous. Was there something about his arrangement with Marguerite that made it dangerous for him to remain with her? Or was he already aware that his superiors were suspicious of his behavior? Later that month, he was arrested on "conduct unbecoming an officer and a gentleman." Perhaps he decided that Marguerite's presence in his life would not help his case. In fact, one of the commanders of the Second Native Guard would later be dismissed from the service for keeping "a woman not his wife" in his quarters.[29]

Daniels may have been on the right side of history when it came to the question of slavery, but he was no gallant hero. Marguerite perhaps initially regarded him as her savior, but she soon learned that he was a notorious womanizer. Before she arrived on Ship Island, Daniels had written in his diary, "The only draw back is the want of a few feminine friends and companions to Christianize our sports. No wonder a man becomes boorish and stupid—Don't catch sight of a petticoat once in three months."[30] Before the war, he had engaged in inappropriate flirtations and liberties with the women of Pointe Coupée Parish.[31] Just a few months after abandoning Marguerite, he took up with the wife of a Confederate soldier.[32]

Marguerite was eighteen years old when she was abandoned by Daniels. She had been enslaved all her life. Only a few months before she had finally tasted freedom, and even that freedom was dependent on providing sexual favors to a Union Army officer. She now had to find a way to fend for herself on the streets of New Orleans. How easy it would have been for her to succumb to despair. Yet, she did not beg, steal, or enter a house of prostitution. Instead, she discovered that she could be her own savior, and she quickly developed a plan that would enable her to survive.

5

ST. MARGARET, KEEPER OF FURNISHED ROOMS

Marguerite Tregre Grossinger

Marguerite, keen on reinventing herself, approached the three-story brick building on the corner of Burgundy and Bienville Streets in the French Quarter.[1] She had formulated a plan. She would become Margaret, a woman capable of earning her own living in one of the toughest cities in the United States. This was no small task in a city teeming with refugees of war, soldiers, northerners seeking economic opportunities, and hundreds of formerly enslaved people in search of refuge.

Perhaps she gained inspiration from St. Margaret of Antioch, a holy figure in the Catholic Church with whom she likely would have been familiar. Marguerite was raised Catholic and remained devout her entire life. St. Margaret would have been significant to her because she bore the English version of her given name. One of the voices the beloved French saint Jeanne d'Arc claimed to hear was that of St. Margaret of Antioch. A painting of St. Margaret done by Raphael also hung in the Louvre, and the Duparcs and Locouls had all been to Paris. Although Marguerite may not have accompanied them, she would certainly have heard all about those trips. St. Margaret had refused to give up her Christian beliefs and was tortured and jailed as a result. While in captivity, she prayed to God to reveal her enemy to her, and a dragon materialized. The dragon swallowed her, and it was in this desperate situation, seemingly without any means of escape, that Margaret made the sign of the cross, a testimony that she still was a believer. The belly of the dragon burst open, and St. Margaret emerged unharmed.[2]

Marguerite had faced many dragons in her past, and in her present circumstances, she was determined to rise unscathed just as St. Margaret had. The Civil War, perhaps the defining event in her life, afforded Marguerite the ability to reinvent herself, yet for a time she was exploited in almost the same manner as on the plantation. Though Marguerite came from a strong Creole background, she chose to reconstruct her identity, calling herself the Anglo names "Margaret" and "Maggie." She embraced a more modern American cultural age, where she could choose her own racial identity and forever cast off the bonds of the plantation.

Despite her seemingly dire circumstances, Marguerite had quite a few factors in her favor. She was young, beautiful, and, as Daniels described, every bit a lady. She was also literate. She had a fine signature, one that could easily have matched that of Flagy Duparc's niece, Odile Carr. The daughter of Duparc's sister-in-law, Odile was raised at the Duparc & Locoul Plantation after the death of her mother, and she was the same age as Marguerite. They would have grown up alongside each other, two beautiful young ladies sharing the same home but in vastly different circumstances. It is likely that Marguerite picked up her literacy skills from Odile.[3] Though it was illegal to teach an enslaved person to read and write, Marguerite, as an enslaved person living within the household, probably observed Odile's lessons. There were even cases in which enslaved domestic were taught to read and write alongside the children of the family, almost on a whim.

The death of her former owner, Flagy Duparc, eliminated a significant threat to her freedom. The seventy-one-year-old former master lay dying of "softening of the brain" at his sister's Toulouse Street mansion in the same neighborhood where Marguerite lived. After suffering what was probably a cerebral hemorrhage, Duparc died on July 26, 1863, and was interred in the family tomb in St. Louis Cemetery No. 1, just a few blocks from Marguerite's residence.[4]

Perhaps the most important advantage Marguerite had was whom she knew. She still had a few connections in French Quarter, and she was determined to use them. Unattached and alone in the city, Marguerite turned to Flagy Duparc's former commission merchant, Romain Brugier. She became a keeper of furnished rooms at 45 Burgundy Street, one of Brugier's tenement buildings.[5] New Orleans in the 1850s was booming, and transients constantly passed through the city on business. They needed a place to stay, so hotels, boardinghouses, and furnished rooms were always full. Hotels and boardinghouses required licenses and had to adhere to certain regulations, whereas furnished rooms did not, making renting them out an ideal occupation for women with limited resources. This was a path particularly followed by women of color. An observer wrote, "Many persons, especially colored women, make it a business to keep furnished rooms or 'chambres garnies.'" He also noted that these provided lodgings only, and restaurants were recommended where meals could be had.[6] An 1867 advertisement for 45 Burgundy Street, the building that housed both a doctor's office on one floor and Marguerite's furnished rooms, appeared in the New Orleans *Times* on January 29, 1867: "FOR RENT—SEVERAL HANDSOMLEY [sic] FURNISHED rooms, with kitchen and servants' room attached. Terms moderate."[7]

The area in which Marguerite was now living—Burgundy Street between Customhouse Street and Bienville—had a reputation for debauchery. When geographer Richard Campanella mapped data compiled by historian Judith K. Schafer on illegal sex establishments in antebellum New Orleans, he found that the vast majority in the French Quarter were on Gallatin Street and Burgundy between Customhouse and Bienville—the exact location of the property where Marguerite was keeping furnished rooms.[8] However, many free women of color ran boardinghouses that were deemed perfectly respectable and aboveboard.[9] Historian and author Charles Gayarré wrote that these quadroon women

> monopolized the renting, at high price, of furnished rooms to white gentlemen. This monopoly was easily obtained, for it was difficult to equal them in attention to their tenants, and the tenants indeed would have

been hard to please had they not been satisfied. These rooms, with their large post bedsteads, immaculate linen, snowy mosquito bars, were models of cleanliness and comfort. In the morning the nicest cup of hot coffee was brought to the bedside; in the evening, at the foot of the bed, there stood the never failing tub of fresh water with sweet-smelling towels. As landladies they were both menials and friends, and always affable and anxious to please. A cross one would have been a phenomenon.[10]

Lavinia Miller, a New Orleans free woman of color, supported Gayarré's assertion that free women of color dominated the keeping of furnished rooms. Miller wrote to her aunt in Natchez, "Madame Amie was here last week, and she was on her way looking for another house. The one she had was too small. She wants to rent furnished rooms and now she has found a larger one."[11] Another free woman of color who made her living as a hairdresser, Eliza Potter, also wrote of women who kept furnished rooms in her 1859 memoir:

> The lady next door was colored, and kept elegant furnished rooms. . . . There are numbers here make fortunes, and it is a common thing to have these furnished rooms, and in no mean street either, but side by side with some of the very best mansions are these furnished apartments. They are generally occupied by gentlemen, who take their meals at the St. Charles [Hotel], and sleep in these apartments; and it is not thought anything if the landlady is colored; even to this day it is very fashionable for gentlemen to take their families to these rooms.[12]

One of the men who took a room at 45 Burgundy Street was Charles Grossinger, a dry goods and mercantile clerk in his late thirties. A Hungarian immigrant, he appears to have fled his country after the revolution that occurred there in 1848. He fought in the failed attempt to obtain Hungary's freedom from the Austrian Empire. Along with military officers, soldiers, and government officials, he took refuge in England, where the British government paid their living expenses and then financed their voyages to New York City.[13] According to newspaper accounts at their time of arrival, "They generally seem to be men of high respectability, and, as evidenced by documents which many of them have brought with them, belong to some of the first families in Hungary."[14] On September 1, 1851, the *Picayune* reprinted an article from a Montgomery, Alabama, newspaper, stating,

> Major Preiss, 1st Lieut. Grossinger and 2d Lieut. Schlienger, Hungarian exiles, who served in the late revolution and shared with Kossuth captivity in Turkey, arrived in our city, on their way to New Orleans. . . . They have certificates from Gen. Bem and other distinguished Hungarians. We learn from them that they are destitute of means for the prosecution of their journey. They are gentlemen who have filled honorable stations in their own country, and are proper subjects in their present situation for the kind office of all who have hearts to sympathize with high minded, honorable men, who have forfeited property and country by struggling for political liberty.[15]

Grossinger had no money when he arrived in New York; he then made his way south to New Orleans where he and his fellow Hungarians were "willing to occupy themselves in any way, even manual labor."[16] Grossinger tried his hand first at importing Hungarian wine with a partner named Freund. The enterprise lasted only a few years.[17] Next he went into business with P. R. Mahieu. They opened a dry goods store on Magazine Street: it specialized in selling fabrics like wool and poplin, appealing to the ladies of the neighborhood to examine their stock of "shawls, cloaks, silk mantles, burnous, and pelisses."[18] Unfortunately this venture proved unsuccessful, likely due in part to the advent of the Civil War. Like many immigrants, Grossinger was pressured to join a militia in defense of the city. It appears he enlisted but never actually served, because no dates of mustering in or details of service appear on his record. This might explain the confusion regarding his military service. Many of Grossinger's Hungarian compatriots served in the Union Army during the Civil War. In fact, there was a Charles Grossinger who served in a New York infantry regiment, but this was not the same Grossinger who resided in

New Orleans and ultimately met Marguerite. The New York soldier was a lighthouse keeper with a family in New Jersey; he died in the early 1870s.[19]

As a foreigner, Grossinger seemed to care little about the racial caste system of the South. Forced to flee from his native land, he had experienced the upheaval and turmoil of war, just as did Marguerite. Though still a young man when he was forced out of his country, he carried the trauma of exile. Newspaper accounts said of Grossinger and his fellow soldiers that "they bear the indelible stamp of the battlefield on various parts of their bodies, and . . . one of those youthful patriots has fought in eighteen different battles."[20] As a Hungarian in the nineteenth-century South, he was very much an outsider, just as Marguerite stood outside the increasingly rigid definitions of race and class. In her relationship with Grossinger, Marguerite broke with much of her Creole past. He called her "Margaret" or "Maggie," and it became the name she would use on all written documents for the rest of her life. It is probable that they spoke English to each other, which meant Marguerite's native French Creole would seldom be used in her home. However, Grossinger embraced Marguerite's Roman Catholic religion. The couple attended St. Joseph Catholic Church not far from their home. Her faith was the one element of her past she would not discard.

By 1880, Marguerite was living with Grossinger on Gasquet Street farther up Canal Street from the French Quarter in the area now occupied by the LSU–VA Hospital complex. In this neighborhood of immigrants populated with people of all races, Marguerite was able to construct a new identity. It is unlikely that she would have encountered anyone from her previous French Quarter life on Gasquet or the surrounding streets. The census taker recorded her as "M. Charles," a widowed woman keeping house for "C. Grossinger," a store clerk. Though they did not identify as married, Marguerite adopted the Creole custom of taking her significant other's first name as a kind of nickname or surname.

Most striking of all was her racial identification. Along with her partnership with Grossinger and her move to a new neighborhood, Marguerite had decided to "pass" as white. Daniels's description of her "alabaster" complexion indicated it would not be difficult for Marguerite to conceal her mixed racial background. As a quadroon, three of her four grandparents were white. Perhaps having reached the age of thirty-five and being in a stable relationship, Marguerite felt she was finally able to choose her own identity and shape her future according to her own dictates.[21]

While Marguerite was establishing a new life for herself, Flagy Duparc's sister Elisabeth Locoul had filed a claim against the U.S. government for property taken during the Civil War. Because her father and husband were both Frenchmen, Elisabeth claimed French citizenship and demanded reparations from the government. Witnesses were called to report the events that took place on the plantation during the war. In his testimony, Louis Smith, Duparc's former driver, told the story of Marguerite and Colonel Daniels. When Francis E. Dumas, former major in the Native Guard and a Creole of color, was questioned about Marguerite, her reputation and newfound status as a white woman lay in jeopardy. "Who were the two women slaves of Mr. Duparc?" the attorney demanded. "What is their present address?" Dumas, who lived in the Marigny neighborhood and had certainly continued to encounter Marguerite for at least a decade after the war, could have easily revealed her identity. Instead, he responded, "I don't answer such questions. . . . I am a gentleman, and I expect to be treated as such."[22] Had Marguerite been called to testify, the new identity she had so carefully created for herself would have been lost. Thanks to Dumas's refusal to engage, Marguerite's history with Daniels and her time in slavery could remain in the past. Just a few years later, Dumas moved to Banks Street and lived just a few houses away from the Grices. They were close neighbors and would certainly have been on speaking terms and aware of the comings and goings in each other's households. This also placed Dumas only two blocks away from Marguerite's Gasquet Street home.[23]

Marguerite wasn't the only person close to Dumas who had successfully transitioned into the dominant caste. His first cousin Achille Rivarde III, born in New York City around 1865, was living in Europe, where racial designations were not as important and far more easily discarded. Much was made about Rivarde's ambiguous ancestry. Many Creoles of color who chose to identify as white either allowed this ambiguity to work in their favor or actively fostered it. Newspapers ultimately chose to identify Rivarde as Spanish or occasionally as Spanish and French. His father, Achille Rivarde II, was a musician and music teacher, known as so many Creole musicians were as "Professor." He left New Orleans for New York City, married and started a family there, and then moved to Europe, where his son Achille III received expert instruction in the violin and became a prestigious concert violinist. Yet most people of color in Louisiana, especially those who were formerly enslaved, could not afford to pick up their lives, move far away, and completely start over. Ironically Achille Rivarde's cousin, François Dumas, was one of the few who could have but chose instead to remain in New Orleans and advocate for equal rights.[24]

Another reminder of Marguerite's old life came with the arrival of her mother in her home. Of half-African and half-European ancestry, Armantine would not have appeared to be the mother of a woman who identified as white. Did Marguerite refer to her as her mother to her neighbors and friends?

Armantine's life had also been transformed by the arrival of the Union Army. Finally free from the bonds of slavery and the sexual exploitation that came with it, she married Justin Stuard, the plantation carpenter, shortly after he was mustered out of the army. Justin had served as sergeant in Company K of the 84th United States Colored Infantry. Both Armantine and Justin sought an education and became semi-literate. Unlike her daughter who chose to create a new life in the city, Armantine remained with Justin on the plantation and spent nearly the rest of her life in the close-knit community alongside those with whom she had endured slavery.[25] In 1887, she went to her daughter's New Orleans home, presumably to be nursed through an illness from which she would never recover. She died of a bowel obstruction and was buried at Cypress Grove Cemetery No. 2 later that year.[26]

The most important change in Marguerite's later years was assuming the role of foster mother to the orphaned Grice children. Not much is known about the relationship of the Grices and Grossingers. What was it that motivated the Grossingers to take in this family of orphans? Is it possible that Alice and Marguerite knew each other from their past lives as enslaved women of mixed race? The old steamboating days along the Mississippi River seem to provide an obvious context for their first meeting: probably Marguerite and Alice met aboard a steamboat. In fact, Flagy Duparc's nephew traveled aboard one of the vessels captained by Alice's uncle. While captain of the *Lafourche,* Alice's father made stops up and down "the Coast," the term used for what are now the River Parishes: St. Charles, St. John the Baptist, and St. James Parishes.[27] Marguerite and Alice lived in the same neighborhood and were parishioners at the same church. Perhaps the true bond lay in nearly identical life circumstances. Alice Thomasson Grice was the daughter of a white steamboat captain and an enslaved woman of mixed race. Like Marguerite, Alice began a relationship with a white man and ultimately chose to identify as white. Both had known the bonds of slavery, though under vastly different circumstances.

After living together for at least fifteen years, Marguerite and Charles Grossinger legally wed on July 11, 1894, at St. Joseph Catholic Church.[28] Why did they choose this date to formalize their union? Perhaps they feared they would never again have the chance. Less than a month before their marriage, the Louisiana state legislature passed an anti-miscegenation law, making interracial marriage illegal.[29] And so they decided to get married before the new law became standard practice. During Reconstruction, when their friends the Grices had married, interracial marriages were legal in Louisiana. With the end of Reconstruction, people of color were being stripped of their voting rights, falsely accused of crimes, violently attacked and lynched, and subjected to Jim Crow laws that legalized segregation. The 1890s was a brutal and dangerous decade in which to be a person of color in Louisiana. Marguerite and the Grice children probably chose to identify as white not only because of the opportunities it afforded them but also because of the safety it provided. Joining them on their wedding day were their close friends Alexander Gaal and William Forstall. Both men signed their names as witnesses to the Grossingers' marriage. Gaal, a Hungarian exile and former soldier like Grossinger, and Forstall, a Creole like Marguerite, had married two sisters. Their life circumstances mirrored those of Charles and Marguerite Grossinger. They were part of a small but significant community that would increasingly find itself threatened as the years progressed. Ultimately their children would be left to bear the burden of the choices of their parents and guardians.

6

TEARS IN THE TELLING

Georgina Lombard Gaal

On April 1, 1883, Georgina Lombard arrived at Immaculate Conception Church just outside the French Quarter. She was forty-two years old and a mother of two daughters. She was about to enter into the first legitimate marriage of her life. Her half-brother Paul Heno, long estranged from her, was there to witness her wedding ceremony, an event that seemed to be associated with her return to polite society and a lifting of the scandal that had rocked their family.[1]

On that balmy spring day, Georgina made her relationship with Alexander Gaal legal in the eyes of the law and blessed by the Catholic Church. She had lived with Gaal for around three years, at a home on Common Street near St. Charles Avenue. There he operated an agricultural bureau, engaging in the sale of land and farms as a kind of brokerage. Gaal was not the first man whom Georgina had lived with out of wedlock. Yet, despite choosing to violate the social mores of her time, Georgina was deeply religious, a quality instilled in her by her Creole mother. She had lived with the shame of illicit relationships and illegitimate children and being shunned by her half-brother and half-sister. Their attitude toward Georgina was somewhat ironic, given that their mother had not been legally wed to either of the men with whom she had children, and Marie was then in a common-law marriage with the father of her children. Yet Paul Heno and Marie Heno Forstall, themselves illegitimate, spurned Georgina for not being married to her daughters' father.[2] It was obvious that the Henos longed to uphold the Victorian ideals of respectability and morality. Georgina's behavior—in fact, her very existence—threatened the new identity they were trying so desperately to forge for themselves.

Georgina had grown up just a little over nine blocks from Immaculate Conception Catholic Church, also known as the Jesuits Church, in her grandmother's French Quarter home. Her grandparents, Noel Gaspard Dupuy and Magdelaine Chevalier, had left St. Domingue during the revolution there and were drawn to New Orleans, a French-speaking Catholic city heavily influenced by the culture of the Caribbean. They were among the 15,000 white, free people of color, and enslaved individuals who came to Louisiana between 1791 and 1815 after the slave rebellion turned revolution.[3] Dupuy, a native of Gros-Morne in St. Domingue, was a hero of the Battle of New Orleans. He served as first lieutenant of the 44th Infantry and was cited for gallantry in the fighting that occurred before the actual battle. Despite being severely wounded, he managed to return to his regiment in time for the battle.[4]

Magdelaine Chevalier, Georgina's grandmother, was a free woman of color from St. Marc in St. Domingue. Magdelaine gave birth to a daughter Almaide on November 26, 1815, and brought her to St. Louis Cathedral to be baptized on August 10, 1817.[5] As a white man, Noel Gaspard Dupuy was legally barred from marrying Magdelaine. Instead, he wed Marie Marcelite Durocher in the spring of 1818.[6] Yet, Magdelaine was fortunate to be one of the many free women of color in New Orleans with money and property. She purchased a lot and house on Dumaine Street in 1819. It was a classic Creole cottage with a high sloping roof and four bays.[7] At the age of twenty-one, Almaide Dupuy had a daughter, Georgina. Georgina's father was Leonard Lombard, a native of Beaune, France, who had arrived in New Orleans in 1836.[8] He was a wine merchant and likely traveled back and forth frequently between France and New Orleans. He died on July 15, 1845, in Baton Rouge when Georgina was still months away from her fourth birthday.[9]

Both Almaide and Georgina likely grew up listening to stories about Magdelaine's life in St. Domingue and her flight from the island. Recall-

923–925 Dumaine Street, home of Almaide Dupuy Heno and birthplace of Georgina and Marie. Photograph by Katy Morlas Shannon.

ing her own grandmother's arrival in New Orleans, Creole of color Anita Fonvergne said, "When the Revolution broke out, [my grandmother] was separated from her mother and never saw her again. You see, my mother went one way with the little baby, and her grandmother took her. My grandmother never heard from her. They don't know if she was drowned or killed. They know she must have died someplace because she was to come to Louisiana with them."[10] The experience of being a refugee seeking asylum must have been harrowing for Magdelaine.

Exiles from the Haitian Revolution like Almaide's parents helped reinvigorate the Creole population in Louisiana, enabling it to continue to challenge the Americans. One hundred St. Domingue refugees arrived in Louisiana between 1791 and 1797, followed by two hundred more through 1802, and more than a thousand at the time of the Louisiana Purchase in 1803. When the Spanish forced Haitian refugees to leave Cuba in 1809 and 1810, an additional ten thousand white Creole planters, free Afro-Creoles, and enslaved people came to New Orleans. This dramatically increased the number of free people of color in New Orleans and led to the city being majority Black in the early territorial period. It also reinforced the dwindling Creole cultural hold on the city.[11]

The Catholic Church provided a refuge and place of semi-autonomy for women of color, both free and enslaved; in fact, it was an integrated space in the early nineteenth century. Historian Emily Clark wrote, "Thousands of slave baptisms recorded between 1730 and 1803 in the sacramental registers of the parish church for colonial New Orleans testify to the frequency with which enslaved Africans and their children became Catholics in at least a formal sense." According to Melissa Daggett, "The Catholic Church was viewed as a shelter from the storm. Literally from birth to death, the free people of color had the support of the Catholic Church. Their babies were christened in the Church; they received the holy sacraments; free people of color were married with the Church's blessings; and when they departed from the world, the priests officiated at their funerals." Travelers to antebellum New Orleans noted that women of color were particularly faithful and made up a significant portion of parishioners at Mass.[12] A Union soldier noticed the congregation's racial diversity when he attended Mass at the Catholic church in Donaldsonville in 1863: "Black and white people were all mixed up and so far as I could see were all treated alike."[13]

Women comprised the majority of the free people of color in New Orleans, and many owned property. In 1830s New Orleans, 855 free people of color owned property worth $2.5 million. Some of the wealth enjoyed by free women of color was given to them by their white partners or fathers. Other free women of color were savvy business owners and accumulated property with their earnings. For many, their real estate, cash, and investments were the result of a combination of these two scenarios.

Two days after Marie Magdelaine Dupuy died on September 7, 1848, her will was located and filed. Her eldest daughter, Elizabeth Éspedes, was left a house, lot, and dependencies in the Tremé on St. Ann between Villere and Marais Streets, a property that Magdelaine had acquired in 1834. Magdelaine also remembered her granddaughter in her will. She gave part of the St. Ann Street property, which was separate from the home that Elizabeth Éspedes inherited and was without any buildings, to seven-year-old Georgina. Magdelaine bequeathed her Dumaine Street home to her second daughter Almaide Dupuy but made sure to note that the movable property within her residence, including furniture, linens, and clothing, was not solely left to Almaide. She reserved five cutlery sets and four pairs of bed sheets for Elizabeth. Almaide also received $600 that she had loaned her mother years ago to buy a slave.[14]

Magdelaine also made provisions for the three enslaved people she held as property. The title to Kitty, alias Rose, a thirty-two-year-old *negresse* she had purchased from slave trader John Woolfolk in 1824, was given to Almaide. She added, "I intend and I desire that this clause of my will be respected and executed as far as possible." Lucy, a twenty-one-year-old *mulatresse*, and her son Edouard, an eight-month-old quadroon, would have a different fate. Magdelaine had acquired Lucy in 1828 when she was just a child. She called for Lucy and Edouard to be freed in recompense for the good services rendered to her by Lucy. Almaide and Elizabeth received a clear message from their mother. She stated, "I desire that immediately after my death all the formalities required for the emancipation of the above-named slaves be fulfilled without delay."

Magdelaine's final instructions pertained to her mother Jarotte Peiré. She dictated the following to Adolphe Mazureau, the notary public: "I want my daughters to take the same care of my mother as I took of her. I especially recommend that they have the power to meet her needs and to maintain her." In keeping with Magdelaine's wishes, Almaide took her grandmother into her Dumaine Street home; more likely, Jarotte was already living there, and Almaide made sure to keep her in residence. Magdelaine signed the will with a mark because she was not literate.[15]

Shortly after becoming a woman of property, Almaide began a relationship with the man she would always consider to be her husband. He was a white man who was connected to a family of steamboat captains and clerks. She called him "Charles Heno." However, at that time in New Orleans there was no Charles Heno. No one named Charles Heno appears in baptismal or marriage records, death certificates, probate or successions, newspapers, or other genealogical records from the time. Long after Almaide's death, her daughter Marie Heno identified her father as George Heno.[16] It was likely that his middle name was Charles. As mentioned earlier, it was not uncommon for free women of color and enslaved women to use the middle name of their children's father instead of the name by which they were typically known. He was particularly close to his brother's children, and one named a son George Charles after him, the same "Charles Heno" living at 181 Gasquet Street in 1868.[17] In fact, the horrific steamboat disaster that Marguerite Tregre Grossinger witnessed as a young girl involved George Heno's nephew, Jean Baptiste Heno: the clerk aboard the *Meteor*, Jean Baptiste provided the details about the fire and scene on the levee to newspapers.[18]

George Heno could not legally wed Almaide because she was a free woman of color. City directories, census records, and other legal documents referred to her as Almaide Heno, and in old age, she referred to herself as the Widow Heno. Marie, the first child of George Heno and Almaide, was born in 1850. Their son Paul was born two years later.[19]

Georgina grew up in the Dumaine Street home with her mother and half-siblings, as well as occasional boarders: Almaide sometimes earned a living as a keeper of furnished rooms. Also present in the household were the enslaved people owned by Almaide. According to the 1850 census, she had in her possession a thirty-two-year-old Black woman—likely Kitty, alias Rose; a twenty-eight-year-old mulatto woman, and a sixteen-year-old Black teenager. On July 17, 1856, Almaide added another enslaved woman to her household: Antoinette Jenne, a sixteen-year-old *negresse* whom she purchased from Marie Julie Lambre. Antoinette remained on Dumaine Street for only four years before Almaide sold her to Robert Joseph Ker in 1860 for $1,400. When selling enslaved people, owners were required by law to acknowledge any tendencies to run away or any known illnesses they might have; if they failed to do so, they could be taken to court. These characteristics affected the monetary value assigned to enslaved persons: people paid less for habitual runaways or enslaved people in poor health. Almaide disclosed that Antoinette Jenne was absent two times from her house when she went on journeys without permission.

"But she always returned to her mistress's home and with the product of her labor," Almaide noted. She made sure to point out that she referred to Antoinette as a runaway "simply to shield herself from reproach on the part of the buyer." Unlike her mother, Almaide signed her name in a confident hand.[20]

It was not uncommon for free people of color to own slaves. In antebellum New Orleans, being a slaveholder was not just a status symbol but was also viewed as a necessity. Almaide provided for her family by taking in boarders, and she likely needed assistance to care for the needs of her home, children, and boarders. She had been born into a society in which slavery was a given, an accepted norm, and as a free person of color, she likely would not have seen enslaved people as her equals. That they may have shared a racial background would not have been as significant to her as we might think today. Emma Hoggatt, a free woman of color and wife of a steamboat barber, provides a window into how Almaide might have felt about purchasing enslaved women. In 1857, Hoggatt reported to her aunt, "Now for me to tell you about a woman that Jeff bought today. She seems to be a woman very willing. Says she can make homemade bread, buscuits [sic], pies and do everythin[g] that's wanting about the house and if she suits I will be just fixed wich [sic] I hope she will."[21]

At the time of her birth, Georgina and her family were part of the largest and most prosperous community of free people of color in the nation. The streets, markets, and levees of New Orleans were all dominated by people of African descent. She would not have felt like an outsider; in fact, Georgina would have felt a strong sense of belonging to a thriving community. These Afro-Creoles of mixed race were merchants, tradespeople, doctors, poets, lawyers, journalists, teachers, and real estate developers. However, the many Americans who moved to New Orleans after the Louisiana Purchase responded harshly to its three-caste system of whites, free people of color, and the enslaved. They considered relationships like that of Almaide Dupuy and Charles Heno to be "open and notorious concubinage," even though the couple would likely have married if it had been legal to do so.[22]

By 1860, economic hardship settled over New Orleans with the coming of the Civil War; Georgiana and her family seem to have suffered financial reversals as well. Almaide took out a mortgage on the Dumaine Street home in 1858. She also either sold the enslaved women, or some had died. Only one enslaved woman—a thirty-four-year-old Black woman—remained in her household. Yet Almaide was able to purchase land in the Tremé in 1864, paying $1,350 for a lot on Roman Street. Later that same year, on December 1, just a couple of weeks before her twenty-third birthday, Georgina became a mother and subject to the stigma of engaging in "open and notorious concubinage." Aline Dupuy, born in the midst of war, was recorded as a "colored" female in the register of New Orleans births. Her father, Charles Dupuy, was a white traveling salesman dealing in liquor and wine. A year or two later, Georgina began living with him. She gave birth to her second child, Corinne, in 1870.

Charles Dupuy's identity is cloaked in mystery. Was he related to Georgina's grandfather's family, the Dupuys? When did he die? Later, Corinne would say that Georgina told her he died when she was very small. Georgina's half-brother Paul claimed to have never seen him and knew nothing of him. Paul went on to say, "It was because of the birth of these two children that her family broke off with [Georgina] and for many years and up to the present neither I nor her other relatives had anything to do with her." This is curious because Georgina appears in the 1870 census as living with her mother and siblings.[23]

Georgina remained in possession of her grandmother's legacy until after the Civil War. She paid the tax bill for 23 St. Ann Street, located in square number 168 in Tremé, to the Freedmen's Bureau's superintendent of education. At the time Georgina was in possession of real estate valued at $600 and of horses and mules also assessed at $600. Unfortunately, because of the loss of relevant documents and the fact that the property no longer exists—it is now the upper part of Louis Armstrong Park—it is difficult to say how Georgina came to lose ownership of 23 St. Ann Street. It appears that the property was sold at auction in 1865. This would indicate that although Georgina may have had enough money to pay a tax for education, she did not have the means to settle all her taxes with the city and state.[24]

By 1880, Georgina and her daughter Corinne were living with Alexander Gaal on Common Street, less than ten blocks from Immaculate Conception Church. She had known him for several years before living with him. Georgina believed that Gaal had been married once before. "I heard my husband in conversation with a countryman of his, Mr. Grossinger," Georgina recalled, mentioning Charles Grossinger, Marguerite's husband, "say he had had a wife in the old country who died before he came to the U.S."

Alexander Gaal, who was born in or around Budapest in the early 1830s, had served in the military in Hungary, first: as a corporal in the imperial army and then, after deserting, becoming a lieutenant fighting for his country's freedom in the Hungarian War of Independence. After being seriously wounded, he fled to Turkey. He was told there that if he returned home he would not be arrested. Yet after going back to Hungary, he was captured and conscripted into the Austrian Army. He then married a woman in Poland, but she died only a few months later of tuberculosis. While fighting with Polish revolutionaries in 1863, he was taken prisoner by the Russians, who turned him over to the Austrians. They agreed to release him only if he would accept exile.[25]

Fleeing conflict in Europe, Gaal arrived in the United States during the Civil War. In October 1864, he enlisted in the Union Army and was named captain of Company F, First Florida Cavalry. In his later application for a federal pension, Gaal described his time in the military and how he came to be disabled. His company had been engaged in a raid in the Florida woods and was ordered to form a *tirailleur* line on horseback. *Tirailleur*, a French term, refers to light infantry trained to engage in skirmishes ahead of the main column. An experienced soldier, Gaal "made certain remarks against the absurdity of such an order" to his major. Yet he was forced to carry out the order. He described the battle:

> My company went too far, especially the left wing being in advance too much. To correct this, I rode as fast as it was possible, between the trees and bushes. At that occasion my horse stepping in a hole, tumbled over and threw me down over his neck. I fell on my back to the ground at full length, felt pain in my right side in the joint, also pain in my right ear

and a sound like buzzing of bees and bled from my mouth and nose. The blood I mostly swallowed, some I spit out, and some I wiped off. Mounting my horse again after a while, I set after my men and was joined by my bugler near the tirailleur line.[26]

In his application for a pension for disabled soldiers, Gaal wrote that his fall from a horse left him with a hernia and deafness. A few days after arriving at Camp Barancas, he broke out in a high fever and soon became jaundiced as well. "It weakened me to such an extent that I not only could do no service, but I hardly could stand on my feet," he recalled. "They called it swamp fever, but I believe it was typhoid." No longer able to serve, he was told to seek a change of climate and was sent to New Orleans to be discharged. Too weak to travel northward, he had to stay in New Orleans, where he was tended to by Dr. L. Kormendy. Gaal stated that at the time most of his hair fell out.

Gaal reinvented himself in the United States. He engaged in various careers and endeavors in attempts to acquire a fortune. In 1870, he was farming at Morganza in Pointe Coupée Parish. Two years later he was back in New Orleans, and prompted by interest from dramatic and gymnastics clubs, as well as private individuals, he opened a fencing school on Canal Street above Dolbran's College. Illness forced him to give it up. He moved Uptown, where he went into the poultry and fruit business and gardening; however, "on account of business reverses and not being able to work with the spade and hoe," he had to "give it up." In 1878, he did a brief stint as a schoolteacher in Assumption Parish. In his pension application, Gaal described his next venture: "In 1880 at the organization of the 'German Union Veterans,' a charitable institution composed of honorably discharged soldiers and sailors of the U.S. Army, German speaking, elected [me] to be the presiding officer of the association." Because of this new position, he remained in New Orleans, where he was working in the agricultural brokerage at the time of his marriage to Georgina.[27]

Unfortunately, the stable and upright lifestyle Georgina longed for was short-lived. Alexander Gaal was appointed to serve as a clerk in the state senate in 1884. After that job ended, he became a vendor for the Louisiana

State Lottery Company. This proved to be Gaal's undoing. He gambled away most of his money and did not provide for Georgina and her daughter. Eventually Georgina had to run a boardinghouse to survive. When the charter of the Lottery Company expired in 1893, Gaal was without a job and was left financially dependent on his wife. One year later, after purchasing land in Jefferson Parish, he asked Georgina to accompany him to Grand Isle, an isolated beach resort on the Gulf Coast south of New Orleans. Georgina, worn down by the strain of providing for her husband, was beginning to show signs of ill health and told him she could not go. He left her at rented lodgings on Conti Street, where she and her daughter Corinne kept furnished rooms and took in boarders to make ends meet.[28]

At the same time as Georgina's marriage was dissolving, her eldest daughter prepared to wed. On February 24, 1892, Aline married Erwin Hanmer, a white man from Illinois. Witnesses at the ceremony were Aline's stepfather Alexander Gaal and her uncles Paul Heno and William Forstall. From that time on, she and her children would be listed as white in all legal documents. In April of the following year, Georgina became a grandmother with the birth of Wendell Hanmer. Over the next four years, Aline had three more children: Juanita, Erwin, and Hazel. Juanita died of spinal meningitis when she was just five months old and the family was living with Georgina on Conti Street. When her youngest child was just three months old, Aline suffered from kidney stones so severely that she died. It is likely that Georgina cared for her grandchildren until her health declined so badly that she could no longer raise them. Her three surviving grandchildren were then given to relatives to raise. All three ultimately moved to the northeastern United States. Their spouses and children were unaware that they descended from a family of free people of color in New Orleans.[29]

Alexander continued to live in Grand Isle until disaster struck. On September 21, 1909, a Category 4 hurricane made landfall there and then moved inland to New Orleans, leaving devastation in its path. At least 350 people were killed by the fifteen-foot storm surge, though this is likely a low estimate of the death toll. Five thousand people lost their homes. Gaal survived but was left with only the clothes on his back. He moved to the isolated fishermen's village at Barataria and took up with a woman named Juanita Messner, whom many assumed to be his wife. In fact, she began to refer to herself as Mrs. Alexander Gaal. Gaal told a pension agent for the government that he intended to divorce Georgina, but he never took the necessary steps to do so.[30]

Meanwhile Georgina continued to eke out a living keeping furnished rooms, taking in boarders with her unmarried daughter Corinne. In 1900, she and her daughter Corinne were identified by the census taker as white women. Georgina told the census taker that her father was born in France, which was true, and that her mother was born in Spain, which was not true. It was a common assertion to make when trying to justify a tan complexion and deny any African ancestry. A lodger from New York was also living with them at the time. After Georgina suffered a stroke and became paralyzed, Corinne took charge of caring for the boarders. By 1910, both mother and daughter appeared in the census with the designation "mulatto," exhibiting the racial fluidity that had existed in New Orleans since its earliest days.[31]

Alexander Gaal died on February 29, 1912, while living on Tulane Avenue with Juanita Messner. He was buried in Chalmette National Cemetery among other Union veterans. His oldest and best friend, Major General Julius Stahl, had passed away just a few months before. In Stahl's will, he left Georgina $500. This would have been a significant boon for an impoverished woman suffering from paralysis. However, Georgina may not have been the intended recipient. Juanita Messner, who was living with Gaal at the time of his death, had Stahl's address and had been corresponding with him. In fact, many people believed Juanita to be Gaal's legal wife.[32]

Juanita provided the pension examiner with the explanation Gaal had given her for his separation from Georgina. "He said he had been deserted about 1894 by Georgina while he was laid up blind temporarily," she said. "He felt very bitter toward her on that account. He felt he was entitled to a divorce from her on that account. He often spoke of applying for divorce from her and of marrying me, but he never did." Conrad Konselman, a friend of Gaal, stated in his deposition that he believed Juanita to be Gaal's real wife and referred to Georgina as the "colored woman downtown" whom Gaal had lived with. As late as 1942, a woman living at Lake Catherine, presumably Juanita, was referring to herself as the widow of Captain Alexander Gaal.[33]

Despite Juanita's claims, Georgina knew that as Gaal's legal widow she was entitled to a pension from the government. A federal pension agent was assigned to her case in the summer of 1912. He interviewed Georgina, her friends, and her family members, including her half-brother Paul Heno, to ascertain whether she was truly Gaal's widow and so could be eligible for a pension. When he visited her at her new home on St. Ann Street in the French Quarter, Georgina's health had seriously deteriorated; she was paralyzed and housebound. The agent described her as being "practically in the shadow of death" and "very religiously inclined." He noted that Georgina had "suffered a severe paralytic stroke and one whole side is helpless.... She can't move about unassisted and her mind and memory are affected to some extent. She is very poor indeed and she and her unmarried daughter seem to have no other income or means of support than by the keeping of rooms." When asked whether Corinne was Gaal's daughter, Georgina explained that her children were illegitimate, that she had never been married before, and that her only marriage was to Alexander Gaal. The agent wrote that Georgina "spoke with the reluctance of shame about this liaison and I believe has told the truth. Both she and her daughter, a seemingly modest young woman, were affected with tears in the telling of this matter." When Corinne was questioned about her stepfather, she stated, "The only trouble was his habits were bad. He was a gambler and would not help my mother."[34]

In his report to the Bureau of Pensions, the agent presented what he had learned about Alexander Gaal:

[He] was a well educated man of the type of person exiled from Europe because of political troubles. I learned he was rather prominent in politics here in carpetbag days [Reconstruction] and later he was a gambler and a lottery ticket seller when New Orleans was a wide open town. Later when the lottery was outlawed he sold tickets for a while surreptitiously. And later in life he was very feeble physically.... All his old friends or most of them seem to be dead.... Soldiers old intimate of the keno and gambling days are dead.

It was 1912, and by this time his closest friends Major General Stahl and Charles Grossinger had both died.

Georgina's testimony confirmed Gaal's penchant for gambling and his inability to provide a stable home: "He would not provide for me. I had to support himself and me by working and keeping boarders on Conti Street between Royal and Bourbon Streets. I asked him to help me and he would not. And so he quit me and we never lived together again. He came only once to see me and that was several years after we parted and then he came only once and told me goodbye and said he was going to Grand Isle and I never saw him again. He was a great gambler and bad provider." Almost everyone the pension examiner interviewed noted Gaal's gambling habits and refusal to financially support Georgina. She was deemed to be his widow and so began receiving a pension.

Georgina began to suffer from her final illness in July 1917. Dr. A. Ledoux attended her for the next several months. She had another stroke on September 26 and died on October 5, 1917, just a few blocks away from where she was born. The death certificate listed her age as seventy, when in fact she was seventy-six.[35] This is consistent with the fact that throughout her adult life she had claimed she was several years younger than she actually was. The doctor reported her cause of death as chronic interstitial nephritis, or kidney disease. He charged Corinne $75 for attending her mother. She wrote to the Pension Bureau asking to be reimbursed for some of the cost, because Georgina was receiving a widow's pension at the time. Georgina also had insurance through P. J. McMahon & Sons Undertaking Company valued at $110. Corinne arranged the service with the funeral directors and embalmers at McMahon. Georgina wore a robe and silk veil at her funeral and was surrounded by candles. A black hearse carried her to her grave. Three carriages conveyed family members.[36] That three carriages were needed suggests that Georgina's half-siblings Marie Heno Forstall and Paul Heno also attended the funeral.

Georgina had spent her entire life in New Orleans, never leaving the city except for a few short visits to the beach resort town of Pass Christian, Mississippi. She had gone from being the daughter of a free woman of color and property holder to a penniless widow abandoned by her husband, all the while straddling the color line. Georgina's story contained complexities her sister Marie would desperately seek to avoid but ultimately could not escape.

7

SCRATCH THE SURFACE

Marie Heno Forstall

Marie Heno Forstall longed for respectability, security, and societal approval and sought to gain it by embracing Victorian mores and rejecting elements of her past. Yet she never hid her past from the man she loved. By 1880, William Forstall, the man she considered her husband, was living with her, her mother Almaide, and her brother Paul and his family. Forstall informed census takers that Almaide was his mother-in-law and Paul his brother-in-law.[1] The family was quintessentially Creole in what was becoming an increasingly American city. They spoke French and worshiped in the Catholic Church, and their families had been in Louisiana for generations. Paul Heno was a printer for *L'Abeille,* also known as the *New Orleans Bee,* the French-language newspaper favored by Creoles.[2] Marie was born and raised in the French Quarter. And William Forstall, as his cousin's obituary would note, was "a representative Creole."[3] Yet their Creole identities would be questioned by the elite whites who regained power after the end of Reconstruction.

The traditional social strata fell apart after the Civil War with the emancipation of enslaved people. Whites wanted desperately to distinguish themselves from Blacks and create a clear hierarchy. People of color who had been free before the Civil War and people of mixed race complicated this effort. White Creoles could no longer tolerate their siblings, aunts and uncles, and cousins of color; to them this group posed a threat to their supremacy as whites. And so attacks against people like Marie Heno Forstall, Marguerite Tregre Grossinger, and Georgina Lombard Gaal intensified. For the first time, the word "Creole" was used as a racial distinction. The old Creole hierarchy based on phenotype, proximity to whiteness, and class had given way to the American racial caste system.

For example, noted historian and writer Charles Gayarré, in a lecture titled "The Creoles of History and the Creoles of Romance" delivered at Tulane University in 1886 and later published, declared that Creoles were of noble and ancient blood and had absolutely no African ancestry. In response to George Washington Cable, a local color author who wrote openly about Creoles of color and relationships that crossed the color line, Gayarré and other powerful white Creoles spent the 1880s and 1890s on a white supremacist campaign against Creoles of color.[4]

"Creole means the issue of European parents in Spanish or French colonies," Gayarré asserted. To be Creole was "to possess a sort of title of honor—a title which could only be the birthright of the superior white race." In case anyone would question this claim, Gayarré elaborated, stating that a Creole was

> a native of European extraction, whose origin was known and whose superior Caucasian blood was never to be assimilated to the baser liquid that ran in the veins of the Indian and African native. This explains why one of that privileged class is proud to this day of calling himself a Creole, and clings to that appellation. . . . It has become high time to demonstrate that the Creoles of Louisiana, whose number to-day may approximately be estimated at 250,000 souls, have not, because of the names they bear, a particle of African blood in their veins.

In fact, Gayarré denied the existence of people of mixed race in Louisiana, citing the Black Code as preventing any such amalgamation:

> It raised Alpine heights, nay, it threw the Andes as a wall between the blacks, or colored, and the natives of France, as well as the natives of Louisiana, or creoles. There could be no marriage between the two races. If a

white master had a child by a slave, that master was to be punished by the infliction of a heavy fine, and was even liable to any other arbitrary punishment by a court of competent jurisdiction according to the circumstances of the case. The slave and child were confiscated and adjudicated to the hospital nearest to the place where the offence was committed.[5]

Gayarré's lecture was farcical: his own life experiences disproved his assertions. On August 3, 1825, Delphine Lemelle, a free woman of color, gave birth to his son. This cannot be disputed: on May 5, 1826, Père Antoine of St. Louis Cathedral baptized the child and recorded that his grandparents were Carlos Estevan Gayarré and Marie Ysavel Boré, parents of Charles Gayarré.[6] Historian Marcus Christian was well aware of Gayarré's hypocrisy. "Gayarré called upon [George Washington] Cable to call family names when he accused the high Creoles with having consorted with negro women, Indian squaws, and French women of ill repute," Christian wrote. "Here it is necessary to state that it was not a very urgent matter for Cable to call family names. If Gayarré had really wanted his hearers to know facts, he could have begun by making a clean breast of things and admitting then and there that he himself was the father of a child by a colored woman."[7] Marie Heno Forstall and Georgina Lombard Gaal likely knew him, because Gayarré was their neighbor. Almaide Heno's Dumaine Street property was described as "bounded on the Burgundy Street side by Mr. Charles Gayarré."[8] At times, Almaide kept furnished rooms to earn a living. As noted in a previous chapter, Gayarré provided the explanation of what it meant to be a keeper of furnished rooms, having observed his neighbor's goings-on over the years.

Gayarré's close friend, author Grace King, published what he wrote. She became a champion of Gayarré, assisting him in his old age. King despised women of mixed race and painted them as villains and seductresses. Perhaps this was the only way she could be reconciled to the fact that her beloved Gayarré had fathered the child of an enslaved woman. Gayarré's speech denounced children like his and people like Georgina, Marguerite, and Alice Thomasson.

White women's hostility toward women of mixed race was nothing new. In 1825, a woman calling herself "Mother of a Family" wrote in the *New Orleans Gazette* complaining of "the insolence of the mulatto girls, who drive the white women from their walks." She referred to them as "Heaven's last, worst gift to white men" and declared that "the purity of Louisiana is threatened, because so delicate and white has the mixture become, that it is absolutely introduced among the wives and daughters of the citizens."[9] Women from St. Domingue like Marie Chevalier, Georgina and Marie's grandmother, were vilified. New Orleans priest Father John Olivier wrote the bishop in 1812, "This city is inhabited by numerous strangers from every country without religion, without customs, and what has put the peak to scandal is the arrival of a very great number of girls of color from Santo Domingo who spread corruption everywhere." In her thesis on Creole women of color, Natasha L. McPherson noted that "interracial concubinage" was a "common practice in colonial St. Domingue." With the arrival of a large refugee population from St. Domingue made up primarily of women, New Orleans saw an upsurge in interracial liaisons. McPherson explained that this was an "immediate and practical response to the conditions of resettlement as white and colored émigrés tried to create stable lives in their newly adopted city."[10]

In New Orleans, interracial liaisons were not only deemed acceptable for white men and Black women but were also openly practiced. Of course, men in the rest of the South engaged in sexual relationships with enslaved women or free women of color, but nowhere were such relationships more open than in New Orleans. Creole men facilitated courtship with women of mixed race through masked balls organized for the express purpose of finding women of color to partner with. C. C. Robin, visiting New Orleans at the time of the Louisiana Purchase, observed, "Winter is the season of balls . . . there are public balls, both for ladies of quality, which means the whites, and for the colored women. The men go to both." Thus, during the winter social season, Creole men could attend two different sets of balls and meet and become attached to two different sets of women, one white and one Black. Creole men could select a white wife from an elite family and enter into a relationship with a free woman of mixed race at the same time. During his stay in New Orleans, John Latrobe wrote of the French

Theatre, "At the further extremity of it is the house in which the quadroon balls are held—and the ticket to both being the same price, the holder of the ticket to the white ball when tired goes out and exchanges with someone who has been among the ladies of mixed blood, and who gives his ticket to get into the crowd where the taint is moral and not physical." The wives of married Creole men could socialize with other women at their private balls, while their husband could go off to the mixed-race balls and either meet up with their lover or acquire one. Neither woman would ever meet in a public social setting, as Robin pointed out: "The Ladies' ball is a sanctuary which no women even suspected of mixed blood may enter. Not even the most pure conduct or most eminent virtue could wash away that stain in the eyes of these implacable dowagers."[11]

Latrobe attended one of the "Quadroon Balls" and described the experience in his 1834 journal:

> Those who had not were young girls as yet destitute of a keeper, and who it seemed to me shewed their faces as a merchant shews samples of his wares to entice purchasers. . . . I was informed that this ball, by no means exhibited the handsomest, and genteelest of the quadroons. In the first place it was the opening Ball to which it was not fashionable for them to come—and again it was more promiscuous than those balls which they have and where a ticket is not a matter of purchase but of favor. These last are called the Society Balls—and the best quadroon society is to be found at them. There were no white women present; and none of the quadroons wore costume.[12]

Thus, Creole society organized venues of courtship for women of mixed race just as it did for white women of the planter class. At the most elite balls, Creole mothers of mixed race sought white men to partner with their mulatto or quadroon daughters by entering into a relationship known as *plaçage*. Terms like "mulatto," "mulatresse," "octoroon," and "quadroon" were common in Creole Louisiana parlance, "because many families had members on both sides of the color line" In the Big House as well as the slave quarters. Since colonial times, white Creole men had engaged in plaçage, a practice in which they established a woman of mixed racial ancestry in a home of her own, typically in the upper French Quarter, supported her financially, and had children with her. This explains Latrobe's reference to a "keeper" or a white man and the women acting as "merchants," hoping to place their daughters with white men. Having a second family with a free Black woman was quite common for white Creoles; occasionally, these men viewed these women as their wives and their mixed-race offspring as their legitimate children, despite their illegality. Even when Creole men had a "legitimate" white family as well, they often provided for the support and education of their mixed-race children and acknowledged them in their wills.

Creole women, both white and of mixed race, spent the winter social season engaged in established courtship rituals, vying for the protection, financial security, and affection that a white Creole man could provide. Yet only the white Creole women could be legally bound in marriage to white Creole men. The legal prohibitions on interracial marriage forced Creole women of color into seemingly illicit, unsanctioned "concubinage" that many viewed as a kind of prostitution. Latrobe certainly equated the plaçage arrangement to prostitution, stating, "I pity the poor creatures whom the white man's sins makes [sic] infamous, and devotes to prostitution from their cradle." These interracial relationships would lead to conflict between Creole women of both races and cause them to hold degrading stereotypes of each other.[13]

Quadroon balls and plaçage also inspired conflict between white men and women, leading to this exchange between "Frank Plume" and "Lucinda Sparkle" in the *Louisiana Gazette* in 1810. Lucinda's editorial argued for creating more venues for "respectable" courtship of white women and so deterring white men from seeking liaisons with women of mixed race at quadroon balls. She hoped to create an environment that would encourage marriage over concubinage. Yet the male New Orleanian who responded to her letter and signed it as "Frank Plume" pointed out the severe limitations placed on the courtship of white women and the large barriers that existed between white men and women. He argued that these limitations and barriers resulted in a lack of intimacy and the inability to develop even friendship, much less love. The debate that ensued concerned not only interracial sex but also relationships between men and women as a whole and the courtship process. Frank pointed out that limited access, superficial considerations such as wealth and beauty, and society's rigid rules prevented any kind of real relationship from forming between white men and women, leading to Creole men seeking out the company of women of mixed race who did not have the same limitations and strictures imposed on them and therefore were more appealing. Rather than vilifying men or proposing superficial changes such as public walks, he advocated that society embrace a full overhaul of its mores:

> Let her persuade parents to discard their illiberal prejudices and invite young men to their houses, that their daughters may have an opportunity of choosing husbands for themselves, and to abandon the unnatural right of choosing for them, or of holding up as an object of traffic to sell to the highest bidder. Let her persuade young ladies to be more sociable themselves, when in the company of young gentlemen. Let her do all this and I will venture to say we shall no longer see our churches crowded with old maids and languishing lasses nor the company of the *fair belles* deserted for that of the *copper-colored nymphs* (emphasis in original).[14]

Lucinda angrily refuted her opponent's claims. She averred that she knew plenty of smart, sociable young women and expressed astonishment that her one letter advocating public walks should have incited such an attack on women. Recalling Eve and the serpent, she wrote that men have always sought to attribute "all the crimes and vices of the age" to women. "The neglect and inattention of the younger gentlemen to genteel female society, is entirely their own fault," she wrote. "I will venture to say that no young gentleman, who would prefer the company of genteel female society to that of a *Quarteroon ball* . . . but can always find it, and I laugh at such whining simpletons, when they come forward with the puny excuse of not having access to the company of our sex."[15] Arguments over the quadroon balls would be waged for decades more.

Despite these writings about quadroon balls, it appears the phenomenon was greatly exaggerated to the point of myth. Certainly, the supposed system of plaçage did not exist as even scholars described it. As of this writing, not a single plaçage contract between a white man and a woman of color has been found in the Notarial Archives or parish records housed in the New Orleans Public Library. In fact, a significant number of free people of color married other free people of color, entering into legal unions recognized by both church and the state. Historians Kenneth Aslakson and Emily Clark have uncovered evidence that disputes the predominance of plaçage relationships and quadroon balls, showing instead that by 1820 most free people of color tried to marry within their own community. Yet gender disparities in the community of free people of color meant there were not enough free men of color to marry free women of color; the majority of manumitted enslaved people—and, as a result, free people of color—were female.[16] With free women of color outnumbering free men of color three to one, there simply were not enough men for them to marry.

Born into a family of free people of color, Anita Fonvergne was proud of her parents' union. "My mother and father were legally married," she said. "I got my mother's wedding invitation. On my birth certificate, they have 'the legal child of Henrietta Rey and Arnold Fonvergne.'" In contrast, Anita felt ashamed of a relationship she had that resulted in an illegitimate pregnancy. "I wasn't married to the man that I had my daughter from," she admitted. "I was eighteen years old, and I guess I was old enough to know better, but I didn't; and he, he fooled me just like he fooled three other girls in New Orleans . . . it near killed my mother, and it near killed me, but we lived through it." Her daughter said, "My father was a white man . . . he never did anything for me. I don't even remember seeing him."[17] There are echoes of Georgina's experience in the recollections of Anita Fonvergne and her daughter.

Yet there remain too many contemporary accounts of quadroon balls, including the travel writings of Harriet Martineau and Frederick Law Olmsted, to entirely dismiss them. Mary Bernard Deggs, a member of the Sisters of the Holy Family, acknowledged the quadroon balls when she wrote of the order's purchase of the old Quadroon Ballroom on Orleans

Avenue: "Before we bought it, the building was truly a place of sin and bad example." The Sisters of the Holy Family, who were themselves part of the community of free people of color with mixed racial ancestry, would be intimately acquainted with these circumstances. In her dissertation on Creole women in the Tremé and Seventh Ward, Natasha McPherson noted that free men of color counseled young Creole women of color to be wary when attending balls and to reconsider entering into relationships with white men, citing Armand Lanusse's poem "La Jeune Fille au Ball" (The Young Lady at the Ball). Lanusse and his contemporaries were themselves products of interracial relationships, and many had white fathers who provided for their education, as well as other benefits they likely would not have been afforded otherwise. "Even as poets implored women to pursue respectable relationships with men of their own class instead of forming extralegal unions with white men, concubinage had already become a necessary evil in the Creole community, despite the risks and negative consequences," McPherson wrote, citing imbalanced sex ratios among free people of color and other significant socioeconomic issues.

McPherson also highlighted an important fact about the almost mythic quadroon balls: they were private society balls sponsored by mothers of elite Creole girls of color with the intention of securing the best possible matches for their daughters. These exclusive events were attended by only the most elite members of New Orleans society. Most of the free women of color who engaged in this kind of socializing did so at public dances; these balls, advertised in newspapers, were open to white men for a fee. They likely led to the formation of interracial relationships as well, though possibly of shorter duration and without the exchange of significant sums of money and property as with plaçage.[18] Free woman of color Eliza Potter openly wrote this about plaçage:

> These young girls are brought up as particularly as any children in the world; they have the very best education that can be given them, are taught music, dancing and every branch of education necessary to the accomplishment of a lady. They are never permitted to walk out to church or school, or any other place, without a servant after them. When they are

marriageable, they are courted by the gentlemen the same as any other ladies, till it comes to the ceremony; then there is a large party assembled, and the young girl is given away by her father or mother, or both; this is called *placayed* [*sic*]; it is the same in their eyes as marriage, but no license is required. Sometimes they live together till they raise generations; then again, others are like some of the license marriages: they stay till they get tired, and then go, some one way, some another.[19]

In the 1890s, Grace King perpetuated the long-established stereotype that a quadroon woman's sole purpose in life was to entrap white men. In *New Orleans: The Place and the People,* King wrote that quadroon women desired "to rise from a lower level to social equality with a superior race . . . hence an aversion on their part to marrying men of their own colour, and hence their relaxation and deviation from, if not their complete denial of, the code of morality accepted by white women, and their consequent adoption of a separate standard of morals for themselves." In her eyes, they were "a shame and a disgrace," and she condemned them as "the most insidious and the deadliest foes a community ever possessed." King and her contemporaries believed that women like Alice Grice, Georgina Lombard, and Marie Heno had "one great ambition . . . to have their children pass for whites, and so get access to the privileged class. To reach this end, there was nothing they would not attempt, no sacrifice they would not make."[20] King's words clearly reinforced the caste system. She also failed to consider that it would be natural for any mother to want a future for her child devoid of lynchings, Jim Crow laws, and limited educational and economic opportunities; nor did she entertain the idea that many of these quadroon women and their white partners had entered into love matches.

Surrounded by prevalent attitudes like King's, it is no wonder that Marie Heno Forstall sought to rid her life of any trace of impropriety. Her own well-being and that of her husband and children depended on strict adherence to moral and societal codes. It was not that she rejected her family; she dutifully took in her niece Aline's orphaned children when her sister Georgina proved too ill to care for her grandchildren. But Marie believed it her mission to protect her husband and children from the hideous white supremacist ideology embedded in life in Louisiana. She must also have recognized that she embodied the insidious threat to old, elite white Creole families that Grace King and Charles Gayarré went on about, because William Forstall, the father of her children, came from a lineage of "gentlemen possessing noble qualities." In fact, King wrote about the Forstall family and even mentioned William in her book, *Creole Families of New Orleans*, which highlighted the oldest and most prestigious ancestral lines. William's grandparents, Edouard Forstall and Celeste Lavillebeuvre, had six children who "formed what may be called the Forstall dynasty, that reigned over the social and financial world of New Orleans for half a century."[21]

William's parents, Felix Forstall and Heloise DeJan, were connected with all the most influential families in the city. Felix Forstall was the secretary of the Cotton Press company. Placide Forstall, William's uncle, was a well-known cotton factor, merchant, and director of Citizens' Bank with connections to the slave trade. Though William's father did not own a plantation, his siblings and other family members were planters and enslaved large numbers of people. His sister Susanne was the wife of Armand Duplantier, who owned a large plantation in St. James Parish. "The Forstalls lie like a stratum of rich ore under the soil of New Orleans society," King wrote. "Scratch the surface under any prominent name and you tap a Forstall. The vein is pure and true, and it has yielded in the past a good profit to the city." Yet if King had penetrated the surface of her genealogical research, she would have discovered that from the colonial era onward there were Forstalls on both sides of the color line, both free and enslaved.[22]

William Forstall, born in 1838, came of age just before the Civil War but did not prove himself a devoted Confederate. Although his cousins ardently fought a foe they considered invaders, William is noticeably absent from the historical record. However, his brother-in-law Octave served under General Beauregard and was known to have done "gallant service." The Civil War proved too much for William's father Felix, who died in 1864.[23]

During Reconstruction, William worked as a cashier and clerk at various stores. He lived with his mother and brothers in the family's Bourbon

William Forstall, husband of Marie Heno and father of William Forstall Jr. *Times-Democrat*, November 6, 1892, 16.

Street home until he began his relationship with Marie Heno. The couple's first child, Josephine Jeanne, was born on June 5, 1881. Jeanne was followed by her brother William on September 2, 1882. Another daughter, Lucie, arrived in 1884 and son George in 1886. All four children were registered as "colored" on their birth certificates. Meanwhile William maintained close ties with his family and served as a pallbearer at his brother-in-law Octave's funeral in 1886. As was the case in so many Creole families, his brother-in-law also happened to be his cousin.[24]

William Forstall and Marie Heno waited until eight years after the birth of their first child to legally wed. Considering Marie's censorious attitude toward her sister Georgina for having children out of wedlock, this seems curious. More than likely, a priest had married them earlier without a license, enabling Marie to harbor no guilt because their marriage had been blessed by the Catholic Church. With their union thus recognized by the Catholic Church but not by the state of Louisiana, Marie must have felt that she and William were married in the eyes of God and therefore differentiated herself from her sister. This type of marriage had existed since Louisiana's earliest days. There were whispers that Père Antoine, the priest at St. Louis Cathedral, performed such weddings. Sister Mary Bernard Diggs of the Sisters of the Holy Family wrote openly about them in her history of the order: "Dear Mother Juliette Gaudin was also a hero at the bedside of the dying of all colors and conditions. If at the time she came into contact with people of different colors living in a state of mortal sin, she would give them no rest until they had their union blessed by the holy Church of Christ, so as to draw God's blessing."[25]

It is also possible that William waited to legally marry Marie until most of his immediate family had died. His sister Suzanne and brother Arthur both died in 1876. William's mother Heloise Dejan Forstall died in 1884, followed two years later by her brother-in-law Octave. By the end of the 1880s, his brother Paul, living away from the French Quarter in reduced circumstances, was the only sibling still alive.

At first, Marie may have been satisfied with God's blessing, but she would eventually obtain a legal marriage as well. On July 8, 1889, Father F. Rougé of St. Augustine Catholic Church, with a license issued by the city of New Orleans in his hand, joined William Forstall and Marie Heno in holy matrimony. Marie's brother, Paul Heno, and brother-in-law, Alexander Gaal, signed as witnesses. Established in 1841 by free people of color, St. Augustine is one of the oldest Black Catholic parishes in the nation, though originally it was fully integrated with free people of color, whites of various ethnicities, and enslaved individuals worshiping together. It was a fitting place for William and Marie's union. Next to Marie's name on the marriage certificate was the word "colored."[26]

Unfortunately, the Forstall family did not have many years left together. William Forstall died of heart disease on May 20, 1895, at age fifty-seven years. At the time of his death, the family was living on Tulane Avenue in the same neighborhood as Marguerite and Charles Grossinger, and William was working as a cashier at John M. Parker & Co., a cotton commission merchant. As a widow with four children ranging in age from fourteen to nine, Marie did what her mother and sister had done in difficult times: she began renting out rooms. In 1900, her brother-in-law Alexander Gaal was boarding in her St. Louis Street home. She also took in her niece's orphaned children, Erwin and Hazel Hanmer. All were marked white in the census, and to distance herself from her past, Marie told the census taker that her father was from France and her mother from Cuba.[27]

When he was around eighteen years old, William Justin Forstall Jr. began working as a junior clerk at Dreyfous Co. Ltd. on Canal Street. It is quite likely that Charles Grossinger, a clerk for Dreyfous, helped young William Jr. get hired. Located in the Touro Building, the store carried dress goods, silks, linens, ladies' capes, jackets, ready-made suits, embroideries, and laces. By 1905, the Forstall family had left Downtown for the Garden District. By this time William Jr. had risen to the coveted position of clerk at D. H. Holmes, the city's premier department store, and likely commuted to work on Canal Street by streetcar. He was assigned to the dress goods department in 1907. The following year his picture appeared in the newspaper along with other D. H. Holmes employees enjoying the annual dinner of the D. H. Holmes Fire Department. William Jr. had been selected to be a member of the fire brigade from among "the best men in the store": it was quite an honor and an indication that his employer considered him responsible and trustworthy. According to a 1908 newspaper

William Forstall Jr. and the D. H. Holmes Fire Department. *Daily Picayune,* June 14, 1908, 26.

article in the *Times-Democrat*, "Every member of the fire brigade [was] paid a salary, entirely apart from the store's salary, and they are also paid for every alarm they answer, either connected with the store or in the near vicinity. Drills [were] held weekly."[28]

William Jr.'s burgeoning career would certainly have inspired optimism in Marie. For the first time in her life, she was living on the other side of Canal Street, with less chance of being recognized or known. The family's fortunes were rising. She probably looked forward to a time when her children would marry and give her grandchildren. Such pivotal events typically brought joy to a mother. Yet the Forstall family's circumstances complicated events as basic and crucial to the human condition as marriage and birth. She had spent her adulthood determined to reinvent herself and shield her children from prejudice and discrimination, not realizing that bureaucrats with long memories could threaten to destroy a lifetime's work.

8

AN UPRIGHT, HONORABLE EXISTENCE

Marguerite Tregre Grossinger and the Grice Children

Alice Grice entered Greenwood Cemetery and headed toward the aisle dubbed "Clover," where Effie, her beloved sister and youngest of the Grice children, had been interred two years before. Her early death and the doctor's diagnosis of "chronic bronchitis" suggest that the tuberculosis that took her mother's life had also infected her. Dead at the age of thirty, Effie had ended her life in much the same way she had lived it: efficiently, empowered, and with a certainty Alice frequently lacked.[1] Effie had seen to it that a will was drawn up, and she had made arrangements for her own burial. She had always been a planner. It would have pained her to know that, despite her best-laid plans, there was conflict surrounding her death. Their sister Clothilde objected to her will and opened a succession for Effie in Civil District Court. Alice had only just finished settling it that month.[2]

The trouble surrounded the one thing of value that Effie owned: the property on Gasquet Street, now renamed Cleveland Avenue. The modest four-room cottage where the Grossingers raised them after the loss of their parents was in Effie's possession at the time of her death, and Effie had wanted it to go to her sister Alice. Both sisters were unmarried, with little means, and had lived together all their lives. In her will, written on May 24, 1911, Effie stated that in the event of her sudden death she wanted to bequeath to her nephew Walter Evans her horse and wagon and to her "dear Sister Alice Grice every thing else I may possess." She also appointed Alice her executrix. Effie died on June 13, just a few weeks after making her will.[3]

Clothilde went to court and opened a succession for Effie on March 24, 1913. No one seemed overly concerned about Walter Evans's special legacy of the horse and wagon. Walter, their sister Bertha's son, lived with the Grice sisters; he was part of their household, and his work as a driver for a furniture company probably helped support them. The judgment rendered by the court determined that the law and all evidence presented were in favor of Alice, and she was put in possession of all her sister's property. In August, however, their brother James notified the court that he would only release his claims against Effie's estate if Alice paid his sister Clothilde $250. Bertha noticeably had no issue with Alice's inheritance and did not question Effie's will. Perhaps to keep peace in the family, a compromise was reached. Alice gave their sister Clothilde $175. The estate was then settled, and Alice could move on. At forty years old, she had never married and had lost everyone closest to her, except her sister Bertha and nephew Walter, who continued to live with her and help support her.[4]

The Grice children endured further tragedy after the loss of their parents. Charles F. Grice was arrested for breach of trust and embezzlement and was brought to trial in 1895 and 1896. He had been working as a collector for an installment house that dealt in household goods owned by a Mr. Jones. Charles would collect the money from clients, ostensibly to bring to Mr. Jones, but then would pocket the money, and withhold the receipts from Jones. When Jones discovered this, he threatened to fire Charles and possibly press charges. Charles's brother Joseph intervened on his behalf, promising Jones that he would settle the shortages if he kept Charles in his employ. Yet Charles could not help himself. Once again, he began taking the money he collected and spending it. This time Joseph was not in town and could not help him or bail him out of jail.

On August 28, 1897, from his cell in the Orleans Parish Prison, Charles penned a letter to the judge assigned his case, revealing the root cause of the embezzlement. He wrote, "At the time of my crime I was addicted to the morphine habit and was not mentally responsible for my act. I wish to withdraw my plea of not guilty to the charge of embezzlement and plead guilty to the charge of petit larceny if your honor so disposes. During my incarceration I have been completely cured of the morphine habit, and this being my first offence. . . . I ask for clemency and when released promise to live an upright, honorable existence."[5]

Three days later, Charles's plea was accepted, and he was sentenced to four months in prison. Unfortunately, despite his claims, Charles could not control his addiction. On September 22, 1903, six years after his conviction and professed cure, Charles Grice applied to the Civil District Court to be sent to the Fenwick Sanitarium at Abbeville, Louisiana, to treat his "morphine and cocaine habit."[6]

The trauma of the loss of a parent once again haunted the Grices in the latter half of the 1890s. Marguerite Grossinger, the woman who had taken them in and who had become their second mother, grew sick from breast cancer. At the time, the only possible treatment that existed was a radical mastectomy first pioneered by William Halsted at Johns Hopkins University. In 1894, he published a paper describing the process. It involved simultaneously removing breasts, nodes in the armpits, and chest muscles. Though the procedure improved the chances of survival, many women feared being disfigured and refused to undergo it. Even if the radical operation was performed, death was still possible, along with complications that could lead to illness and death, such as lymphedema.[7]

Whether Marguerite endured the procedure remains unknown. She was treated by Dr. George King Pratt, considered by the *Picayune* "among the best known physicians of the city." An article printed on December 15, 1889, provided a detailed description of him: "His tall, powerful form, keen eye, thoughtful brow and skillful hand are welcome in many a sickroom and distinguished in medical circles." He was well qualified for a nineteenth-century physician. He had earned a B.S. degree from Louisiana State University and a diploma from the medical department at Tulane University. He served as the Board of Health's sanitary inspector and then as house surgeon of Charity Hospital. Praised for his "brilliant record," Pratt opened his own private practice in 1880. He was a member of the state board of health, state and parish medical societies, and the National Medical Association.[8] Identifying as a white woman and a member of the middle class, Marguerite had access to quality healthcare for the first time. She was in the best possible hands, yet Dr. Pratt proved incapable of curing her.

Marguerite died of breast cancer on April 20, 1898. In her death certificate, she seems almost unrecognizable from the young girl who was born and raised at what is now Laura Plantation and who made her way to the city so long ago. It reads, "Maggie Grossinger (white) native of this city, aged 49 years."[9] Gone was the Creole girl Marguerite Tregre, born into slavery, her plantation past erased and replaced with her adopted city. She was actually fifty-three years old at the time of her death. Undertaker Jacob Schoen handled her funeral. She was buried in Cypress Grove Cemetery No. 2 next to her mother Armantine.[10]

One by one, the Grice siblings found jobs, married, formed their own households, and had their own children. Yet Alice and Effie remained with the Grossingers, even after Marguerite's death. Charles continued to support them as a dry goods salesman, Alice kept house, and Effie was considered "a boarder" by the census taker, though in truth she was more like the child the Grossingers had never had.[11] When Charles, elderly and infirm, began to show signs that the end was near, Effie went to Greenwood Cemetery and purchased a plot on the Clover aisle for $40. The next day she ordered the removal of the remains of Marguerite Grossinger from Cypress Grove Cemetery No. 2 and paid the associated fees so she could be re-interred in Greenwood Cemetery. One week after she purchased the plot, she gave orders to the sexton to bury her seventy-three-year-old adopted father, Charles Grossinger, there. He had died on August 17, 1905, and the priest from St. Joseph Catholic Church had handled the funeral and interment the following day.[12]

The circumstances of Effie's life after the death of Charles Grossinger resembled those of her mother Alice. A succession was never opened for Alexander Thomasson, yet it was clear that his daughter Alice inherited some property from him. The same was true for Effie. Even though no succession was filed for Grossinger, only six months after his death, Effie, an unemployed orphan girl living under his care for twenty-five years, came into enough cash to purchase the home in which they lived. The Grossingers had always been renters. On February 1, 1906, William Hogan, the owner of 2426 Gasquet Street, now Cleveland Avenue, sold Miss Effie Grice a building and lot for $1,900. The four-room cottage included a kitchen, "sanitary bath," sewerage, and the added incentive of being "rat-proofed."[13]

During Alice's walk through the neighborhood to the cemetery, she would have noticed the many changes that had taken place in her forty years of residence. Just across the street from the Grice's former Banks Street home was the Canal and Claiborne Railroad Company car sheds. Streetcars once pulled by horses during Alice's childhood were now electrified. Straight College, a university for people of color established after the Civil War, still operated directly across the street from the Grossinger home, though in a couple of decades it would merge with Dillard University. St. Joseph Catholic Church, where Alice and her siblings had been baptized and their parents married, had moved several blocks up Tulane Avenue into an impressive new edifice with the longest center aisle in the city. In 1895, during some of the greatest racial tension the city had ever known, the old church became St. Katherine, a parish exclusively for Black Catholics. Until this time, none of the city's Catholic churches had been officially segregated. Catholic Creoles of color had long opposed having churches designated exclusively for "Black congregations," but the archbishop, seeing Black parishioners increasingly unwelcome in parishes, designated to the back rows, and treated as second-class citizens, believed that Catholics of color would turn away from the church in droves. To stop their flight, he decided to establish churches exclusively for Black Catholics. When the old St. Joseph was consecrated as St. Katherine, the "negro church," and the new St. Joseph farther up Tulane Avenue was adopted by all its old white parishioners, the Grices and Grossingers did not hesitate in making the change themselves. After all, they had come to an important decision about their racial identity.[14]

The 1880 federal census classified all the Grice children and their mother Alice as mulattoes. By the 1900 census, two decades later, they were all considered white. They had married white men and women, and their children attended white schools. One could wonder whether they even knew that Louisiana law would have been considered them octoroons, of one-eighth African ancestry. How much had Alice told them of her background? Robert, the eldest, was only eight years old when his mixed-race grandmother died, and the only relative of Alice's with whom they had much contact, her sister Emma, passed as white. Had Robert truly believed his mother was white and from France, as he reported on her death certificate, or was the deception planned by the family? The evolution of the children's birth certificates suggests they were moving in the direction of passing as white. Effie Grice's death certificate also serves as a clue. The chairman of the city's Board of Health and recorder of deaths wrote "colored" beside her name. Had the family's history been entirely buried and unknown, she would have been listed as white, as she appears on all other documents.

In the 1860s and 1870s, a time of optimism for people of color in the South, the Grices did not distance themselves from relatives who might reveal Alice and the children's mixed-race background. When Alice's mother died on August 30, 1867, Charles Grice appeared before the recorder of births and deaths and told him of his mother-in-law's passing. A native of Tennessee, she was around fifty-six at the time of her death on Robertson Street, not far from the Grice's home.[15] During Reconstruction, equality between the races—or at least significant progress toward this goal—seemed attainable. Slavery was ended, Black men could vote, rights of citizenship were afforded to people of color through the Fourteenth Amendment, opportunities in education and government opened up, and the judicial system seemed willing to actually uphold the rights of people of African descent. Yet the end of Reconstruction and the withdrawal of federal troops from Louisiana in 1876 brought about an almost immediate shift back to white supremacy and to government by former Confederates. Creoles with any trace of African ancestry like Alice soon realized that real change in the racial caste system of the South would not occur in their lifetimes, and families like the Grices faced serious decisions about their children's futures.

Louisiana became the battleground for legislation involving segregation and racial identity. In 1891, the Comité des Citoyens was created by Creole activists in New Orleans to challenge the Separate Car Act. The organization planned a challenge to the law by having Homer Plessy, a shoemaker in the Tremé, intentionally break the law. Plessy, a self-described "octoroon," could easily be mistaken for a white man. He bought his railroad ticket "passing" as white and sat in the white section of the car. When asked whether he was "colored," he responded that he was, but he refused to move to the "colored" car, and he was promptly arrested. Plessy's actions not only defied the Jim Crow laws spreading throughout the South but also proved to be a very public example of passing as an act of resistance. Plessy threatened the prevalent notion that there were distinct biological and racial separations by showing that a person could not be racially classified by his appearance. His very existence was a challenge to the ideas of race held by most Americans. In her work on racial passing, Marcia Alesan Dawkins brilliantly analyzed the situation: "The Separate Car Act of 1890, because it sought to solidify dominant racial categories and erase the middle, especially threatened members of the Creole community. Segregation law called for a new *episteme* that would only recognize a black–white racial dichotomy—no ambiguities allowed . . . the Creole community recognized that the Act was part of a larger imposed 'Americanization' of their region and erasure of their culture." The Comité des Citoyens and the Creole community it represented weaponized passing, turned it into an act of resistance, and used it "to challenge white supremacy by undermining the . . . constitutionality of racial categories, and by consequence, the legality of racial segregation."[16]

The Comité des Citoyens' challenge to the Separate Car Act took issue with the legality of assigning race to an individual. Plessy was proof that race was not easily defined. Interracial relationships, of which Plessy and his ancestors were the products, challenged racial categorization and monoracial terminology. Plessy's race could not be determined or properly categorized by the binary racial order present in the rest of the country, and thus he had not broken the law. Albion Tourgée, the leading counsel for Plessy, argued, "How much would it be worth to a young man entering upon the practice of law to be regarded as a *white* man rather than a colored one? Six-sevenths of the population are white. Nineteenth-twentieths of the property of the country is owned by white people. . . . Under these conditions, is it possible to conclude that the reputation of being white is not property? Indeed, is it not the most valuable sort of property, being the master-key that unlocks the golden door of opportunity."

Tourgée questioned the state's right to label one citizen white and the other "colored." He maintained that the denigration of Blackness occurred during slavery, when white people owned Black people. Whiteness afforded them property rights; in fact, they even "owned" their white identities. Plessy's passing amounted to a "theft of identity," taking on whiteness to receive goods, services, accommodations, and property to which he was not entitled.[17]

The court ruled that although the Fourteenth Amendment mandated equality under the law, it did not "abolish distinctions based on color socially or a commingling of the two races." The natural order in Louisiana, the South, and ultimately the nation was segregation of the races and a binary system of racial identification. The ambiguous nature of Plessy's race proved particularly disturbing to powerful white politicians and businessmen determined to maintain white supremacy. People like Homer Plessy, Marguerite Grossinger, and the Grice children "suggest[ed] that the taboo of interracial heterosexual sex must be further contained because it yield[ed] a blackness that [was] not necessarily visible." This "invisible Blackness" meant an individual could gain access to rights, property, and opportunities reserved exclusively for white people. Thus, the Grice children challenged segregation and undermined the notion of white supremacy: their very existence was a threat. They showed that the world did not end when European and African ancestry merged, that the products of these unions were not "defective" or "lacking." By choosing to "pass as white," the Grices were taking back power away from a state and a country that sought to enforce a racial label on them. They refused to submit to the binary definition of race that was being imposed and found that there was no category in which they properly fit. So, they autonomously determined that they would steal back their identities and identify in the way that best served them.[18]

The Grices chose to cross the color line during the era historian that Joel Williamson deems "the age of passing," roughly spanning the years between 1880 and 1925. The rate of passing corresponded with the severity of oppression and discrimination toward Blacks in the South. By the 1890s, at the height of violent racial tension nationally when Jim Crow laws were affirmed by the Supreme Court, establishing segregation as the rule of the day, and lynchings were on the rise, people of color who could appear white had strong motivation to do so. Determining the number of people who crossed this taboo boundary is challenging; it was an act that was inherently meant to be surrounded in secrecy, hidden and, if possible, undocumented. Best estimates indicate that the Grices were among 110,000 people with African ancestry identifying as white across the United States, with a rate of between 2,500 to 2,750 people passing over per year. In Louisiana, with its high population of mixed-race individuals, it is probable that between 100 and 500 people of color "became white" every year from 1875 to the 1890s.[19]

Why would families like the Grices choose to pass? In the South, skin color defined a person's life. Race determined one's social position, access to education, employability, basic civil rights, and even the ability to walk down the street feeling comfortable and free. During this period, people of color were falsely accused of crimes, harassed, and threatened with physical violence. There were restrictions on their attending theaters, eating at restaurants, and participating in certain activities; they were barred entry from many businesses and were subjected to segregation in all aspects of life. They were robbed of their voting rights, demeaned, and treated as second-class citizens. For the Grices, who were only fractionally Black and appeared to be white, passing afforded the only means of social, economic, and political advancement available to them.

Yet, passing took a tremendous emotional toll on those who did it. The loss of family, the denial of the past, and the stripping of identity were painful and psychologically disturbing for many. The act of passing, however, was relatively easy for the Grices compared to some of their Afro-Creole contemporaries. With only one grandparent of wholly African ancestry, they looked as if they were white. They had not been present in the New Orleans Creole community for a century or even decades; they were new arrivals, relatively unknown, and could relocate to areas of the city where they knew no one. The Grices did not have to deny their family; in fact, they had no extended family, only siblings. Their grandmother and mother, considered a mulatto and a quadroon respectively, were dead. Their aunts and uncles, many of whom never acknowledged them to begin with, were either dead or themselves passing. In a port city like New Orleans, with a large immigrant population, they could quickly blend in or reinvent themselves.

A wave of paranoia swept across the South between the 1880s and the 1920s when color dictated identity and people like the Grices were considered a major threat to the racial order. They represented "invisible Blackness," which could easily infiltrate white society and destroy "racial purity." In the minds of southerners at the time, as little as one drop of African blood was damning. Like Homer Plessy, the Grices, though only one-eighth African, were considered "contaminated" and "defective." Earlier in New Orleans, French and Spanish legal and social traditions had engendered a more tolerant attitude toward racial passing and a more complex, nuanced view of race. Yet in the late nineteenth and early twentieth centuries, perspectives on race were hardening. The Creoles of south Louisiana were increasingly adopting the viewpoint of the rest of the South, asserting that to be Creole meant to be exclusively white. They rejected their Afro-Creole cousins, friends, and neighbors and engaged in the virulent racism prevalent at the time. In a place where it was often impossible to tell whether one was white or Black on sight, it became increasingly important to whites to label, categorize, and isolate people of color so as to protect their own racial standing and social positions. Thus, New Orleans moved from a tripartite caste system to a dual caste system. For the Grices, the risks were high no matter what they chose to do. People who passed risked the shame of exposure, destruction of their families, and even violence if discovered.[20]

Less than a year prior to the settling of Effie Grice's estate, Alice and her family's experiences would have been a brutal reminder of those risks. New Orleans politics was rife with factions, the latest being Good Government versus the Ringsters. A few days before a primary election was to be held on September 2, 1912, the *New Orleans Item* received anonymous phone calls stating that Good Government workers, "known to be negroes," would be "shot down like dogs" and killed if they attempted to vote. Indeed, Adolph Bonee, a Good Government worker selected to act as commissioner, was shot and severely wounded by a Sewerage and Water Board foreman at his polling place on Election Day. Before the shooting, Ringsters had visited the Board of Health in search of Bonee's birth record to expose him as "passing" for white. P. Henry Lanauze, the recorder of births, marriages, and deaths, admitted that several men had been in to "ascertain whether Bonee was of negro blood," though he conveniently "couldn't remember" who they were. It soon became clear that there had been a deliberate plot to murder Bonee. Later that afternoon Bonee died at Charity Hospital from a perforated gunshot wound to the abdomen. He was thirty-nine years old. Lanauze made sure to classify him as "colored" on his death certificate.[21]

Alice's thoughts would have likely turned to her older brother Robert's grave. He was in the same plot as James's first wife and her family, not far from where she stood. Thoughts of her brother James, who had been married more than once and always to women of exclusively European ancestry, likely came to her, along with snippets of rumors that became more intense just one month earlier. William Forstall, the son of an acquaintance of theirs, had had his name plastered across the papers for trying to marry a white woman. When he was denied a marriage license by the city's Board of Health, Forstall and his fiancée traveled to Mississippi where they were married without incident. Louisiana law not only barred people of color from marrying whites but it also forbade residents from leaving the state to enter into a mixed marriage and then returning to live as husband and wife.[22]

Alice knew of William Forstall and had known his father of the same name. William Forstall Sr. witnessed the 1894 marriage of Charles and

Margaret Grossinger, performed just as the Louisiana legislature was in the process of criminalizing miscegenation after its being legal for nearly a quarter-century. Like the Grices and Grossingers, the Forstalls were parishioners at St. Joseph's. Buried within the church's baptismal records was an entry for William Forstall Sr.'s wife, classifying her as colored and a daughter of a free woman of color. In fact, the Forstalls' marriage license also referred to her as "colored," not an issue at the time they wed because interracial marriage was legal then. But now their son, who had lived all his life as a white man, though he was technically an octoroon like the Grices, was subject to the new laws, denied the right to marry, and made a victim of the "one drop" rule.

9

A MENACE TO THE PURITY OF THE WHITE RACE

Marie Heno Forstall

In 1913 William Justin Forstall stepped out of the annex building of New Orleans City Hall and looked out on Lafayette Square frustrated but undeterred. He had been denied a marriage license by the New Orleans Board of Health recorder P. Henry Lanauze on the grounds that he was, in fact, of the "negro race." Forstall then demanded to know "on which side of his family there was negro blood." He had known the grandmother whom Lanauze accused of having a "blood taint" and possibly had heard whispers about her past, but he had not expected any of that to obstruct his plans. In fact, Forstall was so determined to wed and so enamored that he summoned his intended, Veronica Vickery, and they headed to the Mississippi Gulf Coast in defiance of Lanauze. Mississippi was the destination for many people denied licenses in Louisiana, as Christian explained: "The contracting parties, if near the Mississippi line, may step over into that state, and the contract is perfectly legal if the 'white' person has not more than one-eighth Negro blood." Under Mississippi law then, it was perfectly legal for William Forstall to wed his fiancée.[1]

Perhaps William Forstall was truly shocked by Lanauze's refusal to issue a marriage license. Well-kept secrets about racial passing were commonplace throughout the country, especially in New Orleans. Yet Lanauze's dogmatic approach did not come out of the blue. Every day that Forstall opened the newspaper, he would have been confronted with news of arrests of people who dared to find love across the color line and with articles about the concerted effort to legislate segregation in marriage and sexual relationships. On July 25, 1908, five years before Forstall's failed attempt to receive a marriage license, the Concubinage Law went into effect in Louisiana, making concubinage "between a person of the Caucasian race and a person of the negro race a felony." If convicted, people who broke this law could be imprisoned "at the discretion of the court" for a sentence of between one month and one year, including the possibility of hard labor. And thus began an onslaught of arrests.[2]

Married people; couples in common-law marriages and monogamous long-term relationships; and those involved in brief, casual encounters—all were targeted under the statewide Concubinage Law. This act was designed to give teeth to the Anti-Miscegenation Law of 1894, which prohibited people of different races from marrying: the issuance of licenses was likewise illegal, and justices of the peace and ministers were prohibited from marrying them. However, people of different races continued to have relationships and live together. The Louisiana legislature, realizing that simply denying the right to legitimize these relationships did not prevent them from happening, sought a means of vigorously prosecuting those who engaged in interracial relationships—thereby deterring them from entering into these relationships in the first place. White supremacists' efforts to stop relationships across the color line ultimately sought to eradicate people like the Grices, Henos, and Forstalls and so preserve and protect white bloodlines from being tainted with racial impurity. These white supremacist views were not considered extreme in Louisiana society: they were held by the majority of white people, who had robbed people of color of voting rights and controlled the state legislature and all governmental agencies.

Eugene Bertrand, the first to be arrested "under the new law [the Concubinage Law] prohibiting members of the white and negro races from living together," went to trial on June 2, 1909. Bertrand and the woman in the case, Odette Duval, had dared to engage in the most stigmatized and reviled relationship in the South—that between a Black man and a white woman. Bertrand and Duval left town to escape the charges: he traveled all the way to New York before being brought back by bondsmen, but Duval remained at large at the time he went to trial. Around the same time, Stanhope P. Turnbull and his wife Charity were indicted under the Concubinage Law, despite having been legally married for eighteen years. The New Orleans district attorney was forced to drop the prosecution because he had no case: the Turnbulls married before the Anti-Miscegenation Law of 1894 went into effect, during the almost thirty-year period between 1868 and 1894 when interracial unions were legal in Louisiana. In a similar case, Joseph Schenkinberger and Celestine Green were arrested for violating the Concubinage Law on April 29, 1912. They had been together for eighteen years and had several children. Unfortunately for them, they married just after the Anti-Miscegenation Law went into effect and thus were subject to the Concubinage Law's provisions. Like the Grices, Grossingers, and Forstalls, these couples were prime examples of what the South most feared and was desperately trying to suppress: loving and devoted biracial families that challenged white supremacist claims. Thus, Schenkinberger and Green and so many like them were doubly persecuted, first by the Anti-Miscegenation Law that denied them the right to marry and then by the Concubinage Law that made their living together or even having a relationship a criminal offense.[3]

The destruction of families, damage to individuals, and psychological ramifications of this law cannot be understated. Its passage led to even more rigorous policing of race, pitting neighbor against neighbor and turning family members against each other. Personal vendettas went from the private arena to the public stage as people sought retribution by turning in neighbors, friends, and family members to the police on suspicion of being in interracial liaisons. Spite led a friend of Olivia and Edgar Bernard to go to the police and claim that Olivia was a white woman. Married for seventeen years and both identifying as Black, the Bernards were forced to stand trial despite Olivia being a "a member of a negro society" who had "associated with negroes" and insisting that she herself was Black like her husband. An individual's right to identify as he or she chose was adamantly denied people in the South, even when that individual was a white person choosing to be Black—a kind of alternative "passing" that would seem to harm no one. The suspicion that a White woman might be in a sexual relationship with a Black man was enough to threaten the social order and became a matter for the police and courts.[4]

For example, an investigation by the police into a complaint made against his stepdaughter on November 4, 1909, led to the discovery that Edward von Buelow, the first cousin of Prince von Buelow of the German Empire, was living in violation of the law. Von Buelow was wedded to Ezilda Duvigneaud, on May 14, 1902, by a judge in Gretna, just across the river from New Orleans. In 1909, the district attorney declared the marriage null because Ezilda was the daughter of Adelard Duvigneaud, a white man, and Marie P. Bechet, a Creole of color. Her parents' marriage was legal, because it occurred between 1868 and 1894, but Ezilda's was not. The district attorney charged von Buelow and Duvigneaud with breaking the Concubinage Law and sentenced them to jail. The case led to sensationalized newspaper accounts containing sentences that would sound absurd to twenty-first-century readers, such as "knowing at the time she had colored blood in her veins, although white in color," the district attorney had ordered the arrest of Ezilda and her husband. Initially, they were not able to pay the bond. Friends and colleagues of von Buelow, who was the inspector of internal revenue for the U.S. Customs Service, bailed him out, leaving him despondent that his wife remained incarcerated.[5]

Overcome with fear that he would be forcibly separated from his wife and children and facing humiliation and disgrace as a result both of newspaper coverage and the upcoming trial, von Buelow turned to suicide. He shot himself in the head in a remote outhouse on the banks of the Mississippi River near Algiers. The forty-nine-year-old father left behind a devoted wife, a five-year-old daughter, and three-year-old son. The day after his body was found, District Attorney St. Clair Adams delivered a statement to a reporter from the *Daily Picayune* outlining the facts of the case. He concluded by saying, "The concubinage law is a good law. It should be strictly enforced. The only objection I have to it is that it does not go far enough." Enforcement of the concubinage law cost Ezilda Duvigneaud

The von Buelows. *Daily Picayune*, November 18, 1909, 9.

her husband's life, her legal title as his wife, her children's legitimacy and inheritance, and her societal status. Such was the price for challenging the caste system of the South.[6]

Two weeks after von Buelow's body was found, a two-year-old girl played in the clerk's office while her parents Octave and Josephine Treadway stood before the judge in Criminal Court and were charged for violating the Concubinage Law. Her younger sister, just a baby, slept in her aunt's arms. The *New Orleans Item* reported, "Immediately following the commitment the father and mother, who may yet be separated, hurriedly walked into the clerk's office, the mother going to the infant and giving it motherly care. The father sat nearby playing with the elder child and occasionally smiling and talking to her." Who had caused such pain and fear in this family and ultimately threatened it with dissolution? The children's paternal grandfather, Octave Treadway's father, had repeatedly filed charges against his son for miscegenation and violating the Concubinage Law. The Treadways had already stood trial twice for this offense in Plaquemines Parish, both of which ended in mistrials. They had moved to New Orleans hoping for a fresh start, but the elder Treadway had pursued them and once again reported them to authorities.[7]

Their attorney Lloys Charbonnet succeeded in their defense by arguing that Josephine Lightell Treadway was not a "negro" but an octoroon with only "a slight strain of African blood." Judge Frank D. Chretien then ruled that "the state must show the amount of negro blood in the veins of the accused." District Attorney St. Clair Adams appealed this decision to the Louisiana Supreme Court. Because the Concubinage Law clearly stated "concubinage between a person of the Caucasian or white race and a person of the negro or black race" was a felony, the Louisiana Supreme Court begrudgingly upheld Chretien's ruling and decided against Adams's appeal. On his return to the city from Baton Rouge, where the case was decided, St. Clair Adams announced that the state legislature would be asked at its next session to amend the Concubinage Law "so that the statute might definitely say what is a negro by fixing the degree of Ethiopian blood that constitutes a negro." As predicted, the state legislature altered the Concubinage Law so that it applied to the "colored or black race."[8]

When William J. Forstall sought a marriage license, he did so as a Creole, a member of the tripartite system of the *ancien regime* that had existed in New Orleans almost since its founding: this system initially recognized whites, free people of color, and the enslaved and, after the Civil War, whites, colored, and "negro." Forstall and his ancestors were operating under the assertion upheld by Judge Chretien that "colored" did not necessarily mean Black. In the Crescent City, there were varying degrees of Blackness, and the concept of race was far more fluid and existed under the lens of self-identity, social identity, and legal identity. This was just the way life was in the tripartite caste system that had been part of Louisiana life since the colonial era.

Three years after Ezilda Duvigneaud and von Buelow's arrest under the Concubinage Law and her husband's subsequent suicide, the issue of her race arose again. During the settlement of her father's estate, the ownership of the property he left was contested by his son with his first wife and by his children with his last wife. Brother of a judge and himself an employee of the court, Adelard Duvigneaud had married three times, twice to white women and finally, during the period in which interracial marriage was legal, to Marie Philomene Bechet, Ezilda's mother. Questions surfaced about Adelard's race. The court's judgment stated, "As to the color of Adelard Duvigneaud, the evidence preponderates in favor of the conclusion that he was of the white race. [His] brother was for several years judge of the Second district court of the city of New Orleans. A former clerk of that court, who had occasion frequently to meet Adelard, who was one of the appraisers of the same tribunal, testified that, although of a dark color, Adelard had the hair and appearance of a white man, and was so considered."

Adelard's year of birth, his family relationships, and associates were all provided as evidence, as well as records such as marriage certificates: they ultimately confirmed that Adelard Duvigneaud was legally white. However, how he interacted socially was a different story. One witness stated, "I don't know whether he was a white man or a colored man, but he always associated with colored people. We would consider a man living that way—that is, as a man and wife—with a colored woman, that they were both of the same race." When questioned directly whether Adelard was a white or colored man, the witness said, "No, I don't know; that is hard to tell; he is white and he is colored." How did Adelard himself self-identify? One of his children, when questioned, admitted that his father had acknowledged the judge as his brother and that the judge was certainly white, yet called into question Adelard's race. When asked whether Adelard was a "colored man," his child told the court, "My father never told it to me, but he told it to my mother, and my father had the privilege of a white man." Meanwhile Adelard's daughter Ezilda, though by law in the state of Louisiana a "colored" person, identified as white and was considered white by society until her arrest.[9]

Similarly, Jean Michel Fortier, a member of an elite Creole family, considered free woman of color Henriette Milon his wife and recognized the children she bore him as his own. Testimony in a court case concerning his granddaughter revealed the complexity of racial identity in New Orleans at the time. In 1899, F. M. Fortier, Jean Michel Fortier's first cousin, did not balk at testifying about familial relationships across the color line. F. M. Fortier told the court that he was well acquainted with his cousin's children and that Jean Michel and Henriette Milon and their children "all lived in the same house, and were reputed and looked upon by all persons knowing them as being one family."[10]

All his life William Forstall had considered himself white. He held a job offered to him because he was white, was a member of white organizations, associated with whites, and voted and received the civil rights afforded to white men at the time. That someone in his family—possibly his great-great-grandmother or even his triple-great-grandmother—had been enslaved was immaterial to him; in fact, it was a reality for many New Orleanians. The Concubinage Law and the Treadway case proved a milestone in Louisiana history, signifying the rejection of the tripartite racial caste system. Nuance was done away with, and fluidity denied. A person in Louisiana could be white or Black: there was no in between. This shift "toward a binary understanding of race," historian Michelle Brittain noted, "reflected [the] changing ideological climate." Issued a marriage license in Mississippi on June 24, 1913, Forstall legally wed there and returned home to New Orleans, where in less than a month he would incur the wrath of P. Henry Lanauze, the dogmatic deputy recorder of births, marriages, and deaths in the Vital Statistics Department of the City Board of Health and the embodiment of the "changing ideological climate" that sought to maintain white supremacy and "racial integrity" at all costs.[11]

Born in 1858, Lanauze was the son of a hardware merchant and was connected by birth or marriage to influential Creoles. His first cousin was the wife of noted historian, author, and folklorist Alcée Fortier. Tracing his genealogy back only a generation or two reveals that his family was very much like most Creole families, including the Duvigneauds, Forstalls, and Fortiers. Relatives could be found on both sides of the color line, and often that line became blurred. His maternal grandmother, Marie Félicité

P. Henry Lanauze, ca. 1876. *Times-Picayune,* April 12, 1936, 27.

Wiltz, had half-brothers and sisters of color. His uncle Adolphe Lanauze, who had been in business with his father, married Henriette Feraud. Her mother, Ann Arthemise Sarpy, was the half-sister of Henriette Delille, a free woman of color who founded the Sisters of the Holy Family, an order that offered education and charity to people of color and the enslaved. Stated another way to underscore and clarify their relationship, Lanauze's aunt was the niece of Henriette Delille.[12] These relationships and the nuance and fluidity that characterized them drove Lanauze to reject the tripartite system of which his family was a part and to become instrumental in destroying any compassion or acceptance that existed between family members across the color line. Lanauze fully embraced the doctrine of white supremacy, and his us-versus-them mentality led to a lifelong and very personal vendetta against those who dared to challenge it.

Lanauze's active and public participation in maintaining white supremacy in New Orleans began when he was just sixteen years old. In 1874 in what became known as the Battle of Liberty Place, the White League—a paramilitary organization comprising ex-Confederates and white supremacists—attacked the police and attempted to overthrow the legally elected Republican state government. Cannons were fired down Canal Street, and chaos and violence consumed the city. Lanauze took part in what newspapers of his era characterized as "the battle which restored white supremacy to the city." Because of his small stature, White League combatants assumed he was younger than his age and did not allow him to fight, but he did follow alongside them as they mounted a cannon to shell the Custom House; later, he aided some of the wounded.[13]

The insurrection was a significant factor in the Republican desertion of the South that ended Reconstruction. Civil rights for Black residents of Louisiana could only be maintained by a military presence, and when the presidential election of 1876 was at stake, Republicans engaged in a quid pro quid deal with southern Democrats. After the Republican presidential candidate was elected, the Republicans ended Reconstruction in the South.

Two years after the Battle of Liberty Place, Lanauze at age eighteen began working as a clerk for the Louisiana State Board of Health. When the state legislature created the office of Recorder of Vital Statistics in 1890, Lanauze filled the position. By the time Forstall walked through his doors, Lanauze had been an employee of the Board of Health for almost forty years and was obsessive in his quest to prevent miscegenation, a component of his job that newspapers presented as a "service" to the community: "His long service and an excellent memory has [sic] made him familiar with the family history of every resident of the city who has been here long enough to have one," including the Forstall and Heno families. He worked from eight in the morning to seven or eight o'clock at night, leaving only for dinner and often returning to his office to continue work until midnight. He was in the office most weekends and on all holidays and never took a vacation. His wedding was scheduled outside office hours, and he promptly resumed work the next day. Only once did illness force him to be absent from the office, and then he had to be carried bodily from his desk.[14]

On February 13, 1912, a headline in the *Daily Picayune* read "BLOOD TAINT. Lanauze Will Prepare List for the Board of Health; To Settle Cases Which Come Up Almost Daily, Where Question Is Raised." The article then warned "people in the city of New Orleans who are passing as white when they know that they have a taint of colored blood in veins" that Lanauze was working on a book containing the names and genealogies of families that intermarried across the color line and were breaking the Anti-Miscegenation Law.

Enraged by William Forstall's Gulfport wedding and several other attempts to evade the recently passed Concubinage Law, Lanauze prepared an affidavit detailing these and several hundred instances and submitted it to District Attorney Chandler C. Luzenberg. In the affidavit, Lanauze railed against "frequent and persistent attempts of light-skinned negroes to marry white women," calling them a "menace to the purity of the white home." He specifically mentioned the case of William Forstall. Lanauze's communication with the district attorney came to the press's attention on Saturday, July 12, and he provided them with a statement when the news broke. Reporters must have had access to the written document, because they both paraphrased and quoted from it. Here are excerpts from Lanauze's statement to the press:

> There is not a street, a place of amusement, school or private residence that has not had the contaminating influence of the white-negro.... The object and intent of the law forbidding the intermarriage of the white and colored races was to protect the white people from being deceived by the negro whose skin was almost white.... A law became necessary to stop the white-skinned negro from gaining social equality with the white race. The white-skinned negro is the social danger, for he seeks to elevate himself by intermarriage with the pure white, regardless of the consequences. He cares not whether nature asserts itself by the birth of a dark-skinned negro baby; nor for the humiliation which surely befalls the family of white people into which he has married. He plans, schemes and deceives, in order to get out of his own class. The black negro as a social equal is repulsive to him; still his ambition is to mingle his negro blood with the white race. He boastfully announces his triumph over the law and invariably seeks to rank above the white people with whom he associates.

This was the view Lanauze held of William Forstall. He advised parents to visit the Board of Health to investigate the race of their children's suitors.

People actually began doing this, and newspapers reported at least one young woman was horrified to discover that her prospective husband was "of the negro race."[15]

The press learned about William Forstall's Mississippi wedding from Lanauze's statement. A reporter from the *New Orleans Item* even sought William out at home, as Forstall stood between the columns on the front gallery of the Jackson Avenue home he shared with his mother and siblings. When the reporter mentioned Lanauze's communication with the district attorney and possible legal ramifications, Forstall replied, "I do not understand the matter. The statements contained in the letter are correct. But I did not marry in Louisiana—I went to Mississippi and I don't see where they have any grounds to bother me about it. I will get me a lawyer and see about the case." Despite Forstall seemingly taking it all in stride, his mother, who had spent most of her life trying to blend in with the mores of white southern society, refused to ignore Lanauze's slander of her family. As Forstall conversed with reporters, Marie Heno Forstall descended the front steps and said, "[My] boy ha[s] always been a good, nice boy, and had never done anything wrong."[16]

The next morning, which was a Sunday, the story was featured in every newspaper in the city. *The New Orleans Item* even considered it front-page news. After quoting the Forstalls, the reporter engaged in the characteristic scrutiny that was always directed to people suspected of being racially mixed. The southern obsession with phenotype was readily apparent in this article. Forstall was described as young and well built, "with skin so light that he could easily pass for a white man." As for Marie, whose skin was darker, the reporter dismissed her as "plainly a negro." Had her race not been in question, such a comment would likely not have been made: in typical southern fashion, once a person's race was questioned, people suddenly started seeing them through a different lens. Fifty years before, P. C. Perret, a Creole planter, had testified in a case concerning a woman's race. "From natural [instinct] he would say she was white, why he feels this to be so he cannot explain," the recorder for the court noted of Perret. "Because a creole of this place, being among colored persons of so many different shades of color from snowy white to jet black and the constant intermingling of races the creole can always detect in a person whether that person is of African origin."[17]

The Creole system of detection was in the process of being displaced by the system of Lanauze and his successors, one far more rigid and based on what was believed to be irrefutable evidence. It was a way entirely foreign to Marie Heno Forstall but one she would be willing to challenge for her son.

10

TEARING DOWN THE BARS

Marie Heno Forstall

By Monday, July 14, 1913, the Orleans Parish government and Marie Heno Forstall were further entrenched in their positions and were determined to take action. One headline read "MOTHER WILL SUE TO PROVE SON WHITE." The article opened with District Attorney Chandler C. Luzenberg announcing that he had ordered a probe of "mixed-marriages." Once the investigation was concluded, he was prepared to prosecute Forstall. In response, Marie Heno Forstall declared that she would bring the issue before the courts and have her son declared white. She had already engaged an attorney, Loys Charbonnet, the same lawyer who had represented the Treadways, after which the state legislature revises the original Concubinage Law to specify that it was illegal for all people of color to cohabit with whites. Charbonnet provided a statement from Marie, saying, "She declares that both she and her son are white. It is true that a marriage license was refused Forstall, but that does not mean that he is colored. His wife is well acquainted with the facts in the case and would have left him had she supposed that he was colored. The fact that she has not done so is evidence that Forstall is white." Marie also claimed that her ancestors were "of foreign birth," which was in fact true, given her St. Domingue connection.[1]

What would Marie's mother and grandmother have thought of her response, especially her insistence that her son's bride's love and devotion were predicated on his being white? All the women in Marie's family had been free women of color who had been in relationships with white men. Marie's husband had certainly been aware of her racial background; the priest wrote "colored" next to her name on their marriage certificate. William Forstall Sr. had not abandoned his wife because she was of mixed race. Quite the opposite: he had knowingly entered into a relationship with her, legally married her, raised children with her, and was her devoted husband until parted only by death. Yet for Marie, it was impossible to imagine a love that could sustain a mixed-race marriage in Louisiana in 1913. She did not believe her daughter-in-law was willing to make the sacrifice. Yet Veronica Vickery knew why Forstall had been denied a license and, instead of refusing to marry him, had accompanied him to Gulfport and gone through with the marriage. It was truly society that most frightened Marie and what it would mean to live as a "Negro" in New Orleans in the 1910s. What was so horrifying about being Black in Louisiana that Marie would deny her ancestors, be willing to lie under oath, and engage in her own deplorable rhetoric surrounding race?

Black men could no longer vote in Louisiana: the 1898 Louisiana constitution had essentially disenfranchised them. Two years later, the state legislature passed eight Jim Crow laws legalizing segregation in all public aspects of life. That same year, Robert Charles, a Black man, shot a white police officer, after which a white mob rioted and attacked Black people across New Orleans. Twenty-eight people were killed and fifty wounded, most of whom were Black. This incident led to talk of a "race war." After the Robert Charles shooting, the subsequent violence, and the passage of Jim Crow laws, the number of lynchings dramatically increased. The Catholic Church decided to end integrated parishes, and Catholics like Marie Heno Forstall were told they must attend parishes only meant for Blacks. The Orleans Parish School Board decided that Black children should only be educated through the fifth grade. The same year that Forstall was denied a marriage license by Lanauze, the state legislature closed Southern University, a Black institution for higher learning. Black people were denied jobs, were more likely to be unemployed than whites, were paid less than their white counterparts, and were typically forced into unskilled labor.[2] If a Black man broke the law, it was unlikely that he would receive a fair trial and would certainly not be judged by a jury of his peers. Black people had to step off the sidewalk if a White person approached, and they were condescended to and insulted, treated as inferior, and often forced to bow to whites' authority. Underscoring it all was the constant threat of violence.

Eugenie Lacarra, a Creole of color living in Downtown New Orleans in 1977, reminisced about this painful time: "I stop to think sometimes, and I wonder how the poor colored people got along. You couldn't work in the department stores, the men couldn't drive a bus, you couldn't work for the telephone company, you couldn't work for the Public Service, so if you didn't do menial labor, or housework, or learn to be a cigar maker, or you weren't lucky enough to get an education to teach, well, you were in very bad luck because then these people had nothing to do. You see, they didn't give the poor colored people jobs."

James Montoya's experience supported this description. He went to work at a printing shop, the only one that employed Black workers at the time. He was hired as a Black man but had an altercation with the foreman and was forced to quit. Later he was hired as white at one of the largest printing companies in the city. "It was against my grain to work as white," Montoya explained. "I didn't like to, and when I did it was because I had to—it was an economic necessity. I had gone to another place that hired negroes but they offered me a salary that was the same thing that I had gotten for doing less."[3]

What Marie Heno Forstall likely wanted most was to keep her children safe and ensure that they would have the best lives possible in a place where white supremacy imbued every aspect of society. Over the course of her lifetime, Marie had witnessed a complete reversal of circumstances for the community of Creoles of color in which she was born and raised. Her whole world had been systematically dismantled. Marie's mother and grandmother had owned property, but Marie and her husband never even owned their own home, and she surely feared the same would be true for her children. Marie, her mother, and her grandmother had all worshiped together with white Creoles and enslaved people at St. Louis Cathedral and other Catholic churches. Now she was not welcome in the sacred spaces where her mother and children had been baptized and received into the Church. Born into a French-speaking world, she became painfully aware that only by rejecting her native tongue could she begin to fit in with the Americanized society that now dominated her hometown. Marie and her mother had both been literate at a time when many women—Creole or American, white or of color—were often uneducated. Now officials were denying people with ancestry like hers access to education. She likely decided that the only way to provide her children with a future even remotely similar to her own past was to "pass" as white, to become a member of the ruling caste.

Arthé A. Anthony conducted extensive interviews with thirty New Orleans Creoles of color of the same generation as the Forstall children and Alice and Effie Grice. According to Anthony, "The oral histories of black Creoles born at the turn-of-the-century indicated that racial passing was a last resort strategy employed by individuals in response to the pervasive racial repression that shaped occupation patterns in the early decades of the century." His interview with Alice Simon Chevalier was particularly telling. "In those days if you were kind of fair you didn't want to be a n——r," Chevalier told him. "That's a bad word to use, but that's the word they used in those days. You would go pass for white and try to get a job as white; you'd work as white."[4]

The same morning that the district attorney announced an investigation and Marie engaged an attorney, Lanauze grabbed a staggering pile of vital record books and took a taxi to police headquarters. He testified before a grand jury and provided proof of the allegations he had made against Forstall and others. Determined to stop the practice of marrying in another state and then returning to live in Louisiana, Lanauze said, "My information is absolutely authentic and is taken from official records. I will gladly welcome any investigation that the district attorney may care to make." One month later, no indictments had been filed, but Marie had engaged her attorney to bring mandamus proceedings against the city Board of Health to have her son's race changed to white on his birth certificate. Charbonnet cited the fact that Almaide Heno's baptism was in the white ledger of the St. Louis Cathedral sacramental records book, that Marie's was in the white register at St. Joseph's Catholic Church, and that the baptisms of all her children were recorded in white baptismal registers at Immaculate Conception Catholic Church and the cathedral. Once again, the reporter chose to comment on the Forstalls' appearance. After mentioning that Jeanne and Lucie Forstall would be involved in the case, the reporter stated that the sisters were "reputed to be remarkably beautiful." The media was looking forward to sensationalizing the seemingly romantic notion of tragic octoroon women doomed to never achieve respectability or honest marriages. Two days later the *Picayune* used the same tactic, printing the Forstall sisters' full names and stating that they "are understood to be exceptionally pretty." Curiously the reporter also mentioned that Marie Forstall would call in the "services of an eminent Orleans ethnologist." Lanauze informed the paper that Marie's birth was registered as "colored" and that she was the child of Marie Almaide Dupuy, a free woman of color. Marie referred to the whole affair as an "error" and noted that the case—and likely these revelations—had "caused great shame and mortification to her and her family."[5]

The Forstall case appeared on the docket of the city's Civil District Court on December 8, 1913. Nothing ever came of it. Lanauze's evidence was damning. The birth, marriage, and death records on file at the Board of Health were too conclusive to be challenged. Gone were the days of multiple witnesses, personal testimonies, the dissection of physical appearance, and the nuanced analysis of the past. Marie had nothing to challenge the indisputable proof in Lanauze's possession. Two months after the Forstalls' failed challenge, the matriarch of the Prados family applied for a mandamus to force the Board of Health to register her children as white; she claimed that their race was falsely recorded as being colored and that the error must be corrected. Lloys Charbonnet served as the Prados family's attorney, and once again the race of a great-grandmother was the significant factor in the case. The trial was front-page news when it was revealed that baptismal records from St. Louis Cathedral had been "mutilated." The great tomes from the cathedral were hauled into the courtroom and given as evidence. There were indications that notations had been erased or tampered with and that baptisms had been pasted into the white book.[6]

LANAUZE FIGHTS FOR RACE PURITY

Has Been Keeping the Records Straight for Nigh Two Generations.

THREATENS A BOOK

Scores Indifference Which Leaves Him on Guard Virtually Alone.

"Hardly a week passes but I refuse marriage licenses to negroes wishing to marry whites," said Colonel P. Henry Lanauze, recorder of vital statistics, yesterday in discussing the mandamus proceedings instituted against the City Board of Health by Mrs. Camille Prados to have the records of the Board of Health changed so as to make the records of the birth of her children appear as white.

"I have been in charge of these records since 1876, and it would be impossible for me to estimate how many such marriages I have prevented. The Board of Health records are the safeguards of the white race against mongrelism, and if it should so result that any court could bring about changes in such records as those which cover this case, it would be useless to keep any statistics at all as to births and deaths. To establish such a precedent would make possible the tearing down of the bars and the black strain would find its way in everincreasing streams into the veins of the white race.

"This question of preserving the purity of the white race is not an easy one, as many of our people seem to think. Individuals of negro blood are continually trying to get by, and only the greatest watchfulness on the part of this office prevents their doing so. I have during the past thirty-seven years collected genealogies of the families which have negro blood in New Orleans, and I now only wait for the leisure to publish this record in book form."

Colonel Lanauze here displayed a large loose leaf index containing the names of the parents and the complete family history of hundreds of persons of negro descent. He has taken a deep interest in the question, because he knows that the security of the white race is being constantly threatened by impostors who would pass as whites.

"The integrity of the white race must be maintained at any cost. It is unfortunate that the sins of the fathers must be visited upon their children, but the preservation of the white man's civilization requires it. It is unfortunate that more attention to this matter is not given by our newspapers and those who are responsible for public opinion.

"If the plaintiff in this case were to produce the birth certificate of herself and husband, or the birth certificates of the grandparents of the parties concerned, that would be sufficient. As the records stand now, they show that C. Prados himself signed the birth declaration in four of the births under dispute, registering them as colored."

Colonel Lanauze here exhibited the records, and turning to those of March 4, 1850, showed where the record of the birth of "Adeda Fortunee Prados, issue of the legitimate marriage of Charles Prados, a native of this city, a f. c. m. (free colored man) with Camille Monroe, a native of Mobile, a free woman of color." Declaration by Jean Baptiste Monier, signed by Recorder P. M. Crozat and two witnesses, S. E. Crozat and Eugene Lacoste.

Under date of Feb. 10, 1852, the birth of "Sylvania Prados, issue of the legitimate marriage of deponent and Camille Monroe, a free woman of color, a native of Mobile, Ala.," is recorded. Record signed by C. Prados. Witnesses, Eugene Lacoste and S. E. Crozat. Four other children were recorded by C. Prados, all as colored, until 1866, when the City Board of Health was under negro domination. The negro recorders did not make any records as to the race of births.

"It seems to me," said the veteran registrar, "the indifference with which this question is considered is criminal. I am doing what I can to keep the strain pure, but it does look as though few of our people are willing to take an active part in a matter of such vital importance to them and their children."

"Lanauze Fights for Race Purity." *Daily Picayune*, February 4, 1914, 4.

Lanauze appeared once again before the press and made it clear this was an issue he would doggedly pursue. He produced a marriage record describing the Prados's ancestors as free people of color and pointed out that the only reason there was any question of the race of the Prados family was because at the time of their births, during Reconstruction, "the City Board of Health was under negro domination" and "the negro recorders did not make any records as to the race of births." Lanauze made it clear that despite that gap he had other records that would corroborate his accusations. He displayed a large index with the names of people "of negro descent" that included detailed family histories, and he expressed a desire to turn it into a book and publish it. "I have been in charge of these records since 1876, and it would be impossible for me to estimate how many such marriages I have prevented," he said of his white supremacist crusade. "The Board of Health records are the safeguards of the white race against mongrelism, and if it should so result that any court could bring about changes in such records as those which cover this case, it would be useless to keep any statistics at all as to births and deaths. To establish such a precedent would make possible the tearing down of the bars and the black strain would find its way in ever increasing streams into the veins of the white race." He went on to explain why he believed his job required constant vigilance and dedication: "This question of preserving the purity of the white race is not an easy one, as many of our people seem to think. Individuals of negro blood are continually trying to get by, and only the greatest watchfulness on the part of this office prevents their doing so. I have during the past thirty-seven years collected genealogies of the families which have negro blood in New Orleans, and I now only wait for the leisure to publish this record in book form."[7]

P. Henry Lanauze died at the age of eighty-two on June 27, 1940. He had been the recorder in charge of vital records in New Orleans for sixty-four years. During his time in the Vital Records Department, he had issued marriage licenses to fathers, their sons, and grandsons. Over the course of his career, he registered more than 500,000 births, recorded 375,000 deaths, and issued 160,000 marriage licenses. He maintained his rabid crusade against people of mixed race until his death. His tirelessness, dedication to what he believed to be "the integrity" of the records and his obsession with "racial purity" would inspire at least one of his successors. His practices and his "race" book would continue as standard procedure.[8]

William Forstall and his wife moved out to Lakeview and lived quietly. He went into business with his brother. Marie died six years after her family's persecution by Lanauze. He made sure to mark her race as "colored" on her death certificate. The Forstall sisters never married, likely to avoid what their brother endured and further humiliation at the hands of Lanauze and the press. The Board of Health, supposedly created to advocate for the wellness of New Orleanians, had in fact come close to destroying the Forstalls and many other families. In the decades to come, things would only get worse.[9]

One year after Lanauze's death, Naomi Drake began to work at the Board of Health. Dr. Prudhomme had taken over for Lanauze but would have a short tenure of only seven years. Inspired by her predecessor, Drake took up Lanauze's persecution of people of mixed race and even appeared to model her career after his, adopting a self-sacrificial and dogged demeanor. By 1949, she had ascended to his position. As the deputy registrar of vital statistics, she believed that "she selflessly and untiringly performed the functions of her office with extraordinary devotion to duty," rhetoric akin to that used by Lanauze. She became an autocrat, ruling over the Vital Records Department and, under the guise of maintaining the integrity of the records, continued Lanauze's policy of refusing to issue birth, marriage, and death certificates to people she suspected of having mixed racial ancestry unless they allowed her to issue them as "Colored" or "Negro." She maintained a list of "several hundred allegedly suspicious names," likely the same list kept by Lanauze that he frequently threatened to turn into a book. These became "flagged names," and when a record was

Naomi Drake. *Alexandria Town Talk,* May 15, 1953, 1.

pulled and discovered to contain a name on the list, it was set aside and "would not be issued until [Drake] had personally cleared such application[s] with respect to the applicant's family blood lines or genealogy."[10]

One of those flagged names had been on the list for many decades. Lanauze had battled one Heno; his successor would take on another. When Eugene Louis Heno's son presented his father's death certificate to be registered at the Vital Records Department, Naomi Drake took issue with it. The son had reported his father's race as "white," but Drake informed him that unless he could "present sufficient evidence to dissuade her" she would change the racial designation on the certificate to "Negro," as well as on the son's birth certificate and on those of several members of the family. Drake deemed the evidence brought in by Heno as unsatisfactory. Appalled by her altering official documents and classifying himself and his family members as "Negroes," he sued Drake. The case went all the way to the State Supreme Court. Though long in her grave, Marie Heno Forstall would have commiserated. Eugene Louis Heno was the grandson of her half-brother. And they shared a common ancestor, George Heno.[11]

George Heno was the son of Pierre Heno, a prosperous butcher, and Marguerite Tonnelier. He was one of many children born to the couple. At the same time Pierre Heno began a relationship with a free woman of color named Agathe Fanchon. Like many Creole men in New Orleans—and white men throughout the South—Pierre Heno had his legitimate white family and his free colored family. He chose to reside with Agathe Fanchon, but he was not content with this arrangement. Ultimately, he decided to travel to France with Fanchon and marry her there. While he was away, his wife in New Orleans died, leaving several minor children, including George. The youngest Heno children petitioned the court to force their father to pay for their support. Pierre Heno claimed an inability to support two households and demanded that his children come to live with him in the "house where he resides," which belonged to Agathe Fanchon. The First District Court, scandalized by the thought of white children, particularly a young white girl, being forced to live with their father's concubine, found in favor of the white Heno children. When the court stated that "their father made them associate and eat with the woman with whom he lives, and her children," they failed to recognize that "her children" were actually their half-brothers and half-sisters.[12]

Like his father before him, George Heno had a relationship with a free woman of color. Between 1834 and 1850, he had at least five children with Josephine Mitaud. Adolph, the last child he had with Mitaud, was born in 1850, the same year as Marie, his first child with Almaide Dupuy Heno. This suggests he ended his attachment to Mitaud and transferred his affection to Almaide Dupuy. Almaide and George Heno had two more children in the 1850s: Paul and Aline, who died in infancy. Adolph went on to marry a woman named Marie Louise Bellau, with whom he had Eugene Louis Heno, whose death record was contested and was still a subject of a lawsuit in 1965.[13]

In the period between 1960 and 1965 alone, as the result of Drake's policy, 4,700 applications for certified copies of birth certificates and at least 1,100 applications for death certificates were withheld. This backlog began to create serious issues for residents of Orleans Parish who needed to enroll their children in public school or obtain life insurance on the death of a family member. Attorneys were hindered in their work, so much so that in 1958 the president of the New Orleans Bar Association amended the Revised Statutes to enable attorneys to obtain certified copies of birth or death certificates as long as there was a "direct and tangible interest" therein. Yet Drake continued to obstruct their efforts, and the Board of Health began to be bombarded with complaints. Not only were people frustrated with her withholding documents but they were also outraged by her manner. Attorney Ivor A. Trapolin encountered difficulty in obtaining a death certificate for the father of his client. Trapolin watched Drake inform his blonde-haired, blue-eyed client that one of her grandparents was recorded as "Colored" in a manner that "bordered on sadism." Drake appeared to "derive pleasure in uncovering the details to [the] unsuspecting, unprepared client." When a father went to get a copy of his son's birth certificate to apply for admission to public school, Drake told him "that she knew everyone born in the parish where his father was born was 'mixed.'"[14]

The myriad complaints, numerous angry attorneys and government officials, and backlog of records led the Board of Health to dismiss Naomi Drake. On May 13, 1965, she appealed to the Civil Service Commission, believing she was unjustly terminated. The commission concluded that Drake's "zealous, compulsive interest in the maintenance of 'the integrity and completeness' of the records of her office . . . became a passion exceeding reasonableness, and thereby provoked unending complaints and a backlash of public resentment." In short, Drake's manner was "incompatible with being a good civil servant." She was described as "inflexible," "dogmatic," and guilty of insubordination. Ultimately it seemed that the Department of Health, the Civil Service Commission, and city officials took issue less with her rabid white supremacy than with her manner and approach. Had Drake conducted herself with more discretion and deference to male authorities, she likely would have been able to continue her defense of the racial caste system. Though many in New Orleans gave a collective sigh of relief to see Drake dethroned, the practice of race flagging did not end with her departure.[15]

The impact of Drake and Lanauze and anti-miscegenation laws permeated New Orleans culture and infiltrated the most personal aspects of family life. After conducting extensive interviews with New Orleans Creoles, Virginia R. Dominguez observed in 1986, "Suspicion is part of everyday life in Louisiana. Whites often grow up afraid to know their own genealogies. Many admit that as children they often stared at the skin below their fingernails and through a mirror at the white of their eyes to see if there was any 'touch of the tarbrush.' Not finding written records of birth, baptism, marriage, or death for any one ancestor exacerbates suspicions of foul play. Such a discovery brings glee to a political enemy or economic rival and may traumatize the individual concerned."[16]

In 1993, the *Times-Picayune* published a series about race relations in New Orleans that included an article about Naomi Drake's reign of terror. It had been almost thirty years since her dismissal, but New Orleanians had not forgotten the impact she had on them. A seventy-six-year-old man who identified as white said, "I was born and raised in New Orleans. I have no birth certificate because of one villainous woman named Naomi Drake. My parents were too scared to go to City Hall to register me. I'll probably die with no birth certificate. I consider New Orleans the most racist society in the U.S.A."[17]

Many Creoles of mixed race chose to leave Louisiana because of the harassment of Lanauze and Drake, the denial of their basic civil rights, limited educational and economic opportunities, and the ever-present threat of violence at the hands of white supremacists. Alma Forstall, daughter of William and Veronica Forstall, began dancing when she was just a toddler. While still a teenager, she started teaching dance classes at her parents' home in West End. Her talent garnered so much attention that she moved to Hollywood and had a career as a dancer in films. Several of Georgina Gaal's grandchildren, the Hanmers, left for New York and

Alma Forstall, daughter of William Forstall Jr. and granddaughter of Marie Heno Forstall. Press photograph in private collection of Katy Morlas Shannon.

seemed to easily shed their Creole identities. Ezilda Duvigneaud von Buelow's youngest daughter escaped the memory of her father's suicide and mother's shame by marrying a famous cameraman of the silent picture era and making New York her home. Members of the Grice and Heno families relocated to the suburbs of New Orleans, a trend mentioned in the 1993 *Times-Picayune* series. "I believe that many of the white people who have a Creole background deny it because the word Creole identifies them with blacks," Tania D. Randolph, a Black woman said. "Many of these blacks with a Creole heritage in their family moved out of the Seventh Ward or New Orleans and into Metairie or across the river, where they are living as white.... I may look Spanish or white, but deep down inside of me I am a black person who recognized my Creole heritage. Creole is not a race, it is a heritage."[18]

The culture of the South was built on the principle that whites and Blacks were inherently different, that one group was superior to the other. Designating Alice and her siblings as "colored" may seem arbitrary and absurd when viewed from a twentieth-century perspective, yet for the Grices, race was not just a social construct: it threatened their identities and their place in society. In fact, the American caste system demanded segregation of races even in death.

A modest coping tomb in Greenwood Cemetery, with soil piled above the ground and held in place by walls, contains the remains of the Grossingers and Effie Grice, all of whom chose to violate the seemingly unbreakable racial code of their time. Alice inherited the tomb on Effie's death. When a purchaser acquired a new lot or vault in Greenwood Cemetery, they were issued a receipt with a statement printed across it in bold red letters: "Lots and Vaults in Greenwood and Cypress Grove Cemeteries sold and transferred only to people of the Caucasian race." Despite that forbidding red warning, Alice was interred with her sister in that very plot when she died more than fifty years later. At the time of her death, she was ninety-three years old and had outlived all her siblings. The world she left would be barely recognizable to her namesake, the first Alice Grice. Steamboats had long disappeared from the riverfront, civil rights activist Martin Luther King Jr. had shared his dream of racial harmony with the nation, and New Orleans schools had begun to slowly, painfully integrate. Yet when Alice's funeral was held on the morning of January 11, 1967, interracial marriage was still forbidden in Louisiana. Five months later, in the landmark civil rights ruling *Loving v. Virginia*, the U.S. Supreme Court struck down all anti-miscegenation laws. Louisiana families like the Grices no longer had to live in secrecy and fear. Yet Alice had already been released from those worldly stigmas. In death, she had discovered she had nothing to hide.[19]

EPILOGUE

On a spring evening in New Orleans at the turn of the twentieth century, an old soldier lay dying. Francis Ernest Dumas's room in a modest sidehall cottage on Louisiana Avenue was far from his native French Quarter.[1] As the minutes that remained in his life ticked away, did he contemplate his glories and his failures?

His son Henry arrived. He had come from his home on Cleveland Avenue, formerly Gasquet Street, where he was the neighbor of Charles Grossinger, a department store clerk and widower, and his adopted daughters Alice and Effie.[2] Did he mention them to his father? And did Dumas reveal that he had known the man's wife and in what capacity? Or did he keep her secret still, even after she was in her grave?

After they had been transferred to Ship Island, Colonel Daniels had sent Francis Dumas ashore on a mission to lead his men in a raid on Pascagoula, Mississippi. When the arrival of Confederate cavalrymen necessitated a withdrawal, Dumas led them toward the safety of the Union gunboat, never imagining that an incident with a Black sentry would cause the Union Navy to seek revenge instead of protecting them. The gunboat opened fire on Dumas and his Black troops, instead of on the Confederates pursuing them. Realizing the desperate nature of their situation, he had thrown himself into the breach, turned his men around, and stopped the Confederate attack, allowing the soldiers to escape. Daniels had praised Major Dumas, noting his "unflinching bravery" and that he was "constantly in the thickest of the fight." None of that mattered to General

Banks. He made it clear that he did not want men of color serving as officers and sought to drive them out by any means necessary. Dumas soon tendered his resignation.[3]

After the war, Dumas became involved in politics, determined to make a difference and secure the rights of formerly enslaved people and people of color. In fact, he came very close to being elected governor of Louisiana. During the 1869 Republican nominating convention, Henry Clay Warmoth defeated Dumas in a runoff by just two votes. Warmoth offered Dumas the second slot on his ticket, but Dumas rejected the idea. He continued to serve in government agencies most of his life as the city tax collector and then as a broker at the Custom House. He watched as the world around him crumbled and as the men with whom he had fought chose to die, rather than exist within the confines of a racial caste system.[4]

Charles Sauvinet had been there on the beach with him that day as they faced gunfire from both the Confederates and white Americans. Son of a Frenchman and a free woman of color, Sauvinet held the distinction of being the longest-serving Black officer in the U.S. Army during the Civil War. He had then served as civil sheriff for Orleans Parish. Twelve years after the South's surrender, when the U.S. government made it clear that Reconstruction had failed and Confederates once again rose to power, Sauvinet committed suicide in his home.[5]

Dumas had done what he could to help his friend Jean Baptiste Jourdain. The son of a white man and a free woman of color, Jourdain had also served in the U.S. Army. For a while he was a detective in the Metropolitan Police. His time in the state legislature, during which he supported the dismissal of a white man from North Louisiana who had killed a Black man, ended with him being accused of bribery, slandered, and defamed by white supremacists. He had also endured economic setbacks. Dumas had hired him as a furniture salesman. But it all proved too much for Jourdain. He walked over to St. Louis Cemetery No. 1, sat down before his family's tomb, took out his pistol, and shot himself in the head.[6]

Aristide Mary, a mixed-race attorney educated in Paris like Dumas, had been a member of the Republican Party with him. Together they had advocated for integration. Mary was a true civil rights activist. He helped found the Comité des Citoyens, the organization behind the *Plessy v. Ferguson* challenge to the Separate Car Act and segregation. He killed himself in 1893.[7] When a New Orleans newspaper covered his death, the reporter wrote, "It is a singular coincidence that many of the very wealthy colored men of this city have taken their own lives."[8] To Dumas it was no coincidence. He knew the reasons why.

Yet he had chosen to live. Suffering from asthma and rheumatism, he finally gave in to the forces working against him. In his final years, in an effort to secure a future for his children, he moved Uptown and never corrected anyone when they assumed he was white. His son and daughters married the children of German immigrants. They all chose to identify as white. Somehow, they escaped the wrath of Lanauze and Drake.[9]

Francis Ernest Dumas died on May 26, 1901. Not a single obituary for him appeared in the city's newspapers.[10]

"Race flagging" continued in New Orleans until 1978, when Dr. Doris Thompson, assistant secretary of the Department of Health and Human Resources, put a stop to the practice. She made it known publicly after she was fired from her position by Governor Edwin Edwards. The Office of Vital Records had maintained a list of 250 names of "white families with partially black ancestry," a list that was likely used by Drake and could be traced back to Lanauze. "If you've got a good Louisiana French name, it's probably on the list," Dr. Thompson said. "If an individual went to get a birth record and the name was on the list, the person was referred to the race clerk, or the genealogy clerk, as it was politely called." People were informed that if they wanted birth certificates they would have to agree to list their races as "Negro" or go to court and fight the designation. At the time, the Office of Vital Records adhered to a 1970 law enacted by the state legislature decreeing that anyone who was more than one-thirty-second of African descent was considered Black, essentially still a "one drop rule." Finally in 1983, Governor David Treen repealed this law.[11]

By the time the law was changed, descendants of Alice Grice, Marie Forstall, and Georgina Gaal did not even realize they had cause to rejoice: they identified as white. Most had no idea that they could trace their ancestry back to an enslaved person or free person of color. When Francis

Dumas chose to take up arms in the Civil War, he made his motivation very clear, saying, "No matter where I fight, I only wish to spend what I have, and fight as long as I can, if only my boy may stand in the street equal to a white boy when the war is over."[12] The only way his son ever gained equality with a white boy was by becoming one. Major Francis Ernest Dumas, the highest-ranking Black officer in the Civil War, left only white descendants. Despite his monumental efforts to overturn the caste system, his descendants only received equality under the law when they chose to abandon their rich heritage and become members of the dominant caste.

"Passing" in both literature and the historical narrative has frequently been viewed in a negative light. But what if the narrative were reframed? In some ways, getting to choose your own race, and thereby circumventing the white supremacist caste system, was an act of resistance. Allyson Hobbs's exploration of racial passing in American life led her to acknowledge passing as a means of resistance: "Passing was an expedient means of securing one's freedom, and in its broadest and most expansive formulations, passing became a crucial means through which African Americans called for the recognition of their own humanity."[13] After an exhaustive study of Creoles and social classification in Louisiana, Virginia R. Dominguez concluded, "The successful passablanc breeds both jealousy and pride in the community he leaves behind. It is a situation to which many have reluctantly resigned themselves. They fault not the individuals who pass but the dichotomous system of classification that forces them to pass. Hence, many colored Creoles protect others who are trying to pass, to the point of feigning ignorance of certain branches of their families."[14] Perhaps it is best to start reframing the language. Instead of referring to people as "passing as white," wouldn't it be more accurate to say they passed into the dominant caste?

Yet "passing" into the dominant caste was an unsustainable practice, one available only to a select few and incapable of bringing about the change so desperately needed. Ultimately stopping miscegenation was impossible. This is proven by the stories of Alice, Marguerite, Georgina, and Marie, stories most Americans did not want told and that many people today would still like to bury. Love does not follow the social construct of race;

in fact, most of these stories illustrate that love "bears all things, believes all things, hopes all things, endures all things." It is imperative that we look more closely at the genealogies of most families in Louisiana—and across our nation—and realize the myriad connections across the abstract color line and the destruction wrought by the American caste system. We are all family, interconnected genetically and historically. Acknowledging this is the first step in dismantling the American racial caste system.

ACKNOWLEDGMENTS

My work at Laura Plantation with owner and manager Sand Marmillion led me to Marguerite. I first encountered her name in a slave inventory. I sensed she was someone important and spent years searching for clues that would shed light on her identity. I knew she was an enslaved domestic, who her mother was, and that she may have been intimately involved with the occupying Union forces during the Civil War. I located an important lawsuit filed by St. James Parish plantation owner Elisabeth Duparc Locoul against the United States through the French Claims Commission. In it numerous witnesses testified to what took place in what is now Vacherie, Louisiana, during the Civil War. Several witnesses spoke of a woman identified by Louis Smith, the enslaved driver of Elisabeth Locoul's brother, as "Margaret Tregre." They said she was enslaved on Duparc & Locoul Plantation. As I looked over the data, I realized that this was the same Marguerite listed in inventories of enslaved people and that she was likely the daughter of Séverin Tregre, the plantation overseer. Marmillion dismissed my conclusions; she was determined to believe that Marguerite was the child of a Duparc or Locoul.

It wasn't until my eight-month-old daughter crawled toward a book I had in a pile on the floor and handed it to me that Marguerite's life began to unfold. I uncovered irrefutable evidence supporting my conclusions. The book contained a study of the Louisiana Native Guard and the transcribed diary of Union officer, Colonel Nathan Daniels. That day I sat on the floor with my baby, speed-read the book, and was absolutely shocked to discover Marguerite within its pages. Marguerite led to Alice, and soon an entire microcosm of late nineteenth-century New Orleans emerged. The research I did to add detail to Marguerite's story and uncover Alice, Georgina, and the Forstalls was done independently in my own time. I discovered Seraphine Haydel's story while still in graduate school in 2004 and have wanted to include her in my work for twenty years.

I began writing what would become this book in November 2018, one month before I gave birth to my youngest child. I have spent the last five years working to see this project become an actual book, finding time to research and write in the margins between my job as a historian and my holy labor as a mother of three children. I stood at Marguerite's grave and promised her that the world would know her story. Over those five years, I faced job changes, a global pandemic, and serious health issues, but my dedication to Marguerite, Alice, Georgina, and Marie was unwavering. I am convinced that they are my guardian angels. When I thought I would never finish, they intervened on my behalf. These words are as much theirs as they are mine.

I am grateful to Sand Marmillion and the late Norman Marmillion for their support and encouragement over my career and the opportunities they have afforded me. Wholehearted thanks go to my friends and colleagues Jari Honora, Jay Schexnaydre, Joseph Dunn, Emilie Gagnet Leumas, Heather Veneziano, and Cybèle Gontar. Jari Honora was always available to listen to my thoughts and offer insights. He is a colleague I greatly respect and admire; more than that, he is a dear friend and a person of integrity and great kindness. Thanks to Tiffany Guillory Thomas, K. J. Perkins, Lolita Villavasso Cherrie, Mark Roudané, Shawanda of the Creole Storypot, Xavier Pierre, and the fabulous Dianne Honoré. I would also like to acknowledge the inspirational work of Jo and Joy Banner of the Descendants Project and their fight against environmental racism. Because of their tireless efforts and extraordinary dedication, the plantation on which Seraphine Haydel Rivarde was born is now protected. Their support of my work means the world to me.

I am indebted to the many outstanding archivists who assisted me in locating and retrieving the hundreds of records necessary to complete this project. Siva Blake, Sybil Thomas, and Beryl Hunter made the Notarial Archives a delightful and warm place to visit and always went above and beyond to find the records I needed. Many thanks to Greg Osborne and Amanda Fallis at the New Orleans Public Library. There will never be enough praise for Dorenda Dupuy and Katie Vest of the archives of the Archdiocese of New Orleans, my favorite place to conduct research. Amy Simon with the Diocese of Baton Rouge's archives came to my rescue at the very end of this endeavor, graciously helping uncover invaluable records.

I truly appreciate the insight of fellow writers who saw early drafts, including Edward Ball and Ruth Laney. I am especially grateful to Jenny Keegan of LSU Press who immediately recognized the importance of this story. Thank you, Jenny, for championing the stories of Marguerite, Alice, and so many others.

I am a writer, researcher, and critical thinker because of my beloved teachers. Christy Paulsell, Jamie Huard, Candyce Watsey, Alice Couvillon, Laura Decker, the late Melanie Plesh, and Laura Callico will forever be in my heart.

My sincere gratitude to Alan Duhé, a descendant of Edwige Duplantier and Jacques Duhé, who connected with me and helped put me on this journey. My heart was so full when Alan first called me "cousin." I am so profoundly honored to be his cousin.

I am especially touched by the encouragement and support of Jodie Phillips Robinson, a descendant of Alice Grice. Her grandfather named her mother Effie in honor of his beloved aunt. The courage, tenacity, and love exhibited by the women profiled in this book and their descendants continue to inspire me.

Carlie Spear, Melody Barnum, and Revé Pounds—you are my touchstones and my North Stars. This book would not exist without you.

Many thanks to my parents Victor François Morlas III and Kathleen Vidrine Morlas, my sisters Holly Morlas Garcia and Amanda Morlas, and my grandparents Victor François Morlas II, the late Jacqueline Bourgeois, Frances Darbonne Vidrine, and the late Julius "Jack" Vidrine. Your love is always with me. Much appreciation to my late great-grandparents, Hendrix Bourgeois and Bertha Duhé Bourgeois, whose memories of St. James and St. John the Baptist Parishes first brought me to the River Road.

Special thanks to the people who believe in me more than anyone else in the world and who have sacrificed the most in helping this project come to fruition: my husband Robin Shannon and my children Evelyn, François, and Theodore. I humbly pray this book will in some small way help dismantle the systems of oppression that plague our nation.

NOTES

Abbreviations

AANO   Archives of the Archdiocese of New Orleans
LSA   Louisiana State Archives, Baton Rouge
NARA   National Archives and Records Administration, Washington, DC
NARC   Notarial Archives and Records Administration, New Orleans
NOPL   City Archives, Louisiana Division, New Orleans Public Library

Translations of French and Spanish documents are by the author unless otherwise noted. All newspapers cited are from New Orleans unless another city is specified.

Author's Note

1. Amrita Chakrabarti Myers, *Forging Freedom: Black Women and the Pursuit of Liberty in Antebellum Charleston* (Chapel Hill: University of North Carolina Press, 2014), 13.

Introduction: Creoles and Free People of Color in Early Louisiana

1. Original Acts, October 20, 1834, #333, and January 1837, #19 and #21, and St. John the Baptist Parish.

2. Federal Mortality Census Schedules, 1850–1880, and Related Indexes, 1850–1880, Archive Collection: T655, Archive Roll Number: 21, Census Year: 1849, Census Place: St. John the Baptist Parish, Louisiana, Page: 645.

3. Records of the Bureau of the Census, Record Group Number: 29, Series Number: M432, Residence Date: 1850, Home in 1850: St. John the Baptist Parish, Louisiana, Roll: 239, Page: 264b.

4. Records of the Bureau of the Census, Record Group Number: 29, Series Number: M653, Residence Date: 1860, Home in 1860: St. John the Baptist Parish, Louisiana, Roll: M653_424, Page: 623, Family History Library Film: 803424.

5. Marriage of Edward Duhé and Vinah Maumus, St. John the Baptist Marriages, January 15, 1891; "Louisiana Deaths, 1850–1875, 1894–1960," FamilySearch (https://www.familysearch.org/ark:/61903/1:1:FSYK-BS7 : Sat Oct 14 01:36:39 UTC 2023), Entry for Edward Duhé and Jack Duhé, 25 Jan 1941; Year: 1870, Census Place: Ward 6, St. John the Baptist Parish, Louisiana, Roll: M593_529, Page: 349A; Year: 1880, Census Place: 6th Ward, St. John the Baptist Parish, Louisiana, Roll: 469, Page: 57A, Enumeration District: 161; Diocese of Baton Rouge, Department of the Archives, (SMI-9, 190), (SMI-10, 5); Partition and Sale of Rights, Titles, and Interests, Charles Fortin et al., Conveyance Records, Book 19, page 538, filed April 16, 1841, St. James Parish Courthouse; Sale of plantation, Armand Duplantier to Charles Fortin, Conveyance Records, Book Z, page 34, filed April 16, 1851, St. John the Baptist Parish Courthouse; Sale of plantation, Fortin et als to Joseph LeBourgeois, Conveyance Records, Book Z, page 211, filed February 11, 1853, St. John the Baptist Parish Courthouse; Joseph Lebourgeois's Mount Airy Plantation Labor Contract, Register and Payrolls of Freedmen Employed on Plantations, Roll 38, page 1, Louisiana Freedmen's Bureau Field Office Records, NARA.

6. Evariste Duhé (Private, Co. H, 76th Lou. Usc. Inf., Civil War), pension application no. 1196397, certificate no. 1002274, Case Files of Approved Pension Applications, 1861–1934, Civil War and Later Pension Files, Department of Veterans Affairs, Record Group 15, NARA.

7. Year: 1900, Census Place: Police Jury Ward 4, Saint John the Baptist, Louisiana, Roll: 580, Page: 9, Enumeration District: 0063; Year: 1910, Census Place: Iowa Ward 2, Johnson, Iowa, Roll: T624_408, Page: 3b, Enumeration District: 0088, FHL microfilm: 1374421; "U.S., School Yearbooks, 1880–2012," School Name: University of Iowa, Year: 1917; Altanette Ford, "Circle of Strength" (master's thesis, California State University, 2016), 75, 76, 77.

8. John McCusker, *Creole Trombone: Kid Ory and the Early Years of Jazz* (Oxford: University of Mississippi Press, 2012), 25, 38, 50, 54, 58, 67, 98.

9. *New Orleans Item*, October 30, 1924.

10. Isabel Wilkerson, *Caste: The Origins of Our Discontents* (New York: Penguin Random House, 2020), 17.

11. Wilkerson, *Caste*, 17–19; Rebecca Scott, *Degrees of Freedom: Louisiana and Cuba after Slavery* (Cambridge, MA: Harvard University Press, 2009). See also Rebecca Scott's work comparing the post-emancipation societies of Louisiana and Cuba. Ultimately, Scott demonstrates that as Louisiana turned away from its Latin roots and adopted the binary racial hierarchy of the United States, it became a hostile society for people of color and led to the rise of Jim Crow legislation and racial violence.

12. Wilkerson, *Caste*, 19.

13. Bradley C. Bond, ed. *French Colonial Louisiana and the Atlantic World* (Baton Rouge: Louisiana State University Press, 2005), 31, 208.

14. Daniel H. Usner Jr., *Indians, Settlers, & Slaves in a Frontier Exchange Economy: The Lower Mississippi Valley before 1783* (Chapel Hill: University of North Carolina Press, 1992).

15. Bond, *French Colonial Louisiana*, 210–214.

16. Richard Campanella, *Bienville's Dilemma: A Historical Geography of New Orleans* (Lafayette: Center for Louisiana Studies, 2008), 21; Gwendolyn Midlo Hall, *Africans in Colonial Louisiana* (Baton Rouge: Louisiana State University Press, 1992), 6, 8.

17. Hall, *Africans in Colonial Louisiana*, 29, 97–118.

18. Hall, *Africans in Colonial Louisiana*, 157–199.

19. Usner, *Indians, Settlers, & Slaves*, 65–70.

20. Thomas N. Ingersoll, *Mammon and Manon in Early New Orleans* (Knoxville: University of Tennessee Press, 1999),148–157.

21. Hall, *Africans in Colonial Louisiana*, 276–315.

22. Kimberly S. Hanger, *Bounded Lives, Bounded Places: Free Black Society in Colonial New Orleans, 1769–1803* (Durham, NC: Duke University Press, 1997); Warren E. Milteer Jr., *Beyond Slavery's Shadow: Free People of Color in the South* (Chapel Hill: University of North Carolina Press, 2021), 77, 110.

23. Campanella, *Bienville's Dilemma*, 33.

24. Walter Johnson, *Soul by Soul: Life inside the Antebellum Slave Market* (Cambridge, MA: Harvard University Press, 1999).

25. Judith Kelleher Schafer, *Becoming Free, Remaining Free: Manumission and Enslavement in New Orleans, 1846–1862* (Baton Rouge: Louisiana State University Press, 2003), 89.

26. Caryn Cossé Bell, *Revolution, Romanticism, and the Afro-Creole Protest Tradition in Louisiana, 1718–1868* (Baton Rouge: Louisiana State University Press, 1997), 77.

27. Joseph M. Flora et al., *The Companion to Southern Literature: Themes, Genres, Places, Movements, and Motifs* (Baton Rouge: Louisiana State University Press, 2002), 617; Marisa J. Fuentes, *Dispossessed Lives: Enslaved Women, Violence, and the Archive* (Philadelphia: University of Pennsylvania Press, 2016).

28. Joel Williamson, *New People: Miscegenation and Mulattoes in the United States* (Baton Rouge: Louisiana State University Press, 1995), 103; Myers, *Forging Freedom*, 4, 49, 56, 57, 120; Alisha Gaines, *Black for a Day: White Fantasies of Race and Empathy* (Chapel Hill: University of North Carolina Press, 2017); Michelle Elam, *The Souls of Mixed Folk: Race, Politics, and the Aesthetics in the New Millennium* (Stanford: Stanford University Press, 2011); Julia S. Charles, *That Middle World: Race, Performance, and the Politics of Passing* (Chapel Hill: University of North Carolina Press, 2020), 87; Allyson Hobbs, *A Chosen Exile: A History of Racial Passing in American Life* (Cambridge, MA: Harvard University Press, 2014), 97–105.

29. Marcus Christian Collection, Mss 11, Earl K. Long Library, University of New Orleans.

Prologue

1. Baptism of Juan Bautista Christophe, son of Ciprien (Simphorien) and Felicite Tagiasco, lists paternal grandfather as Christophe Haydel and grandmother as Angelique, February 17, 1818, (SLC, B 29, 200), AANO.

2. Succession of the Widow Pierre Becnel, Inventory of Goods, 1830, Act 33, Original Acts, St. John the Baptist Parish Courthouse.

3. Glenn Conrad, *Saint Jean Baptiste Des Allemands: Abstracts of the Civil Records of St. John the Baptist Parish to 1803* (Lafayette: University of Louisiana at Lafayette Press, 1992) 1795, No. 37, 38; Charlotte, free *negresse*, emancipation to Simphorian et al., quadroons, Acts of Carlos Ximenes, September 11, 1795, vol. 9, act 406, NARC, New Orleans.

4. Year: 1810, Census Place: New Orleans, Orleans, Louisiana, Roll: 10, Page: 259, Image: 00220, Family History Library Film: 0181355; 1820 U S Census; Census Place: Orleans, Louisiana, Page: 116, NARA Roll: M33_32, Image: 130; Year: 1840, Census Place: New Orleans Ward 3, Orleans, Louisiana, Roll: 134, Page: 188, Family History Library Film: 0009691.

5. Baptism of free quadroon girl, natural daughter of Seraphina Christoval, November 19, 1812, born November 19, 1807 (SLC, B 13), AANO.

6. Acts of Alexandre Emile Bienvenue, March 2, 1853, vol. 6, act 35, NARC, New Orleans; Acts of Alexandre Emile Bienvenue, July 18, 1853, vol. 7, act 129, NARC, New Orleans; Acts of Alexandre Emile Bienvenue, August 16, 1854, vol. 8, act 127, NARC, New Orleans; Acts of Alexandre Emile Bienvenue, June 1, 1858, vol. 15, act 95, NARC, New Orleans; Acts of Alexandre Emile Bienvenue, April 1, 1860, vol. 17, act 110, NARC, New Orleans.

7. Succession of Anais Rivarde Hopkins, opened July 16, 1896, docket no. 50360, Civil District Court, NOPL; Year: 1850, Census Place: New Orleans Municipality 1 Ward 7, Orleans, Louisiana, Roll: M432_236, Page: 374B, Image: 412.

8. Achille Rivarde to Seraphine Haydel, Sale of Slaves, Acts of Notary Charles Foulon, May 23, 1845, vol. 17, act 200, NARC.

9. *Daily Picayune*, May 16, 1846.

10. *Daily Picayune*, March 29, 1848.

11. Marriage of Elisabeth Rivarde and Joseph Dumas, February 24, 1831 (SLC, M 9, 8), AANO.

12. Shirley Elizabeth Thompson, *Exiles at Home: The Struggle to Become American in Creole New Orleans* (Cambridge, MA: Harvard University Press, 2009), 150.

13. Succession of Anais Rivarde Hopkins, opened July 16, 1896, docket no. 50360, Civil District Court, NOPL.

14. Year: 1860, Census Place: New Orleans Ward 6, Orleans, Louisiana, Roll: M653_419, Page: 165, Family History Library Film: 803419; Joseph Dumas to Seraphine Haydel, Sale of Property, Acts of Notary Theodore Guyol, July 8, 1847, vol. 7, act 427, NARC.

15. *L'Abeille*, August 21, 1860.

16. Francis E. Dumas Pension, *Louisiana Review*, November 11, 1891.

17. James G. Hollandsworth, *The Louisiana Native Guards* (Baton Rouge: Louisiana State University Press, 1998).

18. Francis E. Dumas to Major General Hurlbut, March 8, 1865, Union Provost Marshals' File of Paper Relating to Individual Citizens, Record Group 109, NARA.

19. C. P. Weaver, *Thank God My Regiment an African One*, 15.

20. Year: 1840, Census Place: Orleans, Louisiana, Roll: 131, Page: 211, Family History Library Film: 0009691; Seventh Census of the United States, 1850, Record Group: Records of the Bureau of the Census, Record Group Number: 29; Sale of slaves by Achille Rivarde to Joseph Dumas, Acts of Jules Mossy, May 24, 1845, vol. 26, act 161, NARC, New Orleans; Sale of slaves by Achille Rivarde to Mrs. Joseph Dumas, Acts of L. T. Caire, May 2, 1845, vol. 97, act 194, NARC, New Orleans.

21. Mortgage by P. L. & M. A. Becnel, to B. Toledano & Taylor, April 3, 1861, Letters Received by the Office of the Adjutant General, Main series, 1861–1870, Record Group 94, NARA.

22. Armant-Becnel Family Papers, Howard-Tilton Memorial Library, Tulane University.

23. James H. Courshore, ed., *A Volunteer's Adventures: A Union Captain's Record of the Civil War* (New Haven, CT: Yale University Press, 1946), 47–48.

24. Claim No. 695, Elise Lecoul, Record Group 76, Records of Boundary and Claims Commission and Arbitrations, NARA.

25. Claim No. 695, Elise Lecoul.

26. Claim No. 695, Elise Lecoul.

1. The Issue of Her Body: Alice Thomasson

1. *Daily Picayune,* December 26, 1858.
2. *Daily Delta,* December 25, 1858.
3. *Daily Crescent,* December 25, 1858.
4. *Gardner's New Orleans Directory* for 1867 (New Orleans, 1867).
5. S. L. Kotar et al., *The Steamboat Era: A History of Fulton's Folly on American Rivers, 1807–1860* (Jefferson, NC: McFarland, 2009), 165.
6. *New Orleans Daily Crescent,* September 13, 1858.
7. *New Orleans Daily Crescent,* December 25, 1858.
8. *Daily Picayune,* December 25, 1858, December 26, 1858.
9. Leonard V. Huber, "Heyday of the Floating Palace," *American Heritage* 8, no. 6 (Oct 1957).
10. *Thibodeaux v. Thomasson et al.*, No. 4283, 17 La. 353. New Orleans, March 1841. *Thibodaux v. Thomasson et al.*, No. 4719, 1 Rob. 376. New Orleans, February 1842.
11. Year: 1830, Census Place: West Feliciana, Louisiana, Series: M19, Roll: 43, Page: 230, Family History Library Film: 0009686.
12. Year: 1850, Census Place: West Feliciana, Louisiana, Roll: M432_231, Page: 280A, Image: 240.
13. *Thibodaux v. Thomasson.*
14. *New Orleans Crescent,* May 19, 1854.
15. Emerson W. Gould, *Fifty Years on the Mississippi* (St. Louis: Nixon-Jones Printing Co., 1889), 399, 618–619, 683.

16. *Dalfares vs. Maillot,* No. 2897, 9 La. Ann. X, New Orleans, June 1854.
17. *New Orleans Weekly Democrat,* January 25, 1879. This also includes an account of Thomasson's time with Jenny Lind.
18. *Daily Picayune,* August 9, 1880.
19. *Louisville Daily Courier,* February 28, 1851.
20. Gould, *Fifty Years on the Mississippi,* 619.
21. *Daily Picayune,* January 19, 1879.

2. Being Once Free: Alice Thomasson

1. *Daily Picayune,* March 5, 1854, and August 8, 1845.
2. Gould, *Fifty Years on the Mississippi,* 683.
3. Carl A. Brasseaux et al., *Steamboats on Louisiana's Bayous: A History and Directory* (Baton Rouge: Louisiana State University Press, 2004), 173; *New Orleans Crescent,* December 15, 1849.
4. *New Orleans Crescent,* May 14, 1850.
5. *Daily Delta,* June 26, 1851.
6. Records of the Bureau of the Census, Record Group Number: 29, Series Number: M432, Residence Date: 1850, Home in 1850: Cincinnati Ward 6, Hamilton, Ohio, Roll: 689; Page: 89a.
7. Casey Weldon, "Cincy Places: Cincinnati, Ohio River in Underground Railroad," *Spectrum News Cincinnati,* February 23, 2022.
8. Hobbs, *A Chosen Exile,* 97.
9. Weldon, "Cincy Places," February 23, 2022.
10. Records of the Bureau of the Census, Record Group Number: 29; Series Number: M432, Residence Date: 1850, Home in 1850: Cincinnati Ward 6, Hamilton, Ohio, Roll: 689, Page: 89a.
11. Judith Kelleher Schafer, *Slavery, the Civil Law, and the Supreme Court of Louisiana* (Baton Rouge: Louisiana State University Press, 1994), 268–269.
12. Shafer, *Slavery, the Civil Law,* 271–274.
13. Shafer, *Slavery, the Civil Law,* 274–275.
14. Shafer, *Slavery, the Civil Law,* 275–279.
15. *Philadelphia Inquirer,* January 20, 1879.
16. *Daily Picayune,* November 18, 1884; Calvin Schermerhorn, *Money over Mastery, Family over Freedom: Slavery in the Antebellum Upper South* (Baltimore: Johns Hopkins University Press, 2011), 73–74.
17. *Fayetteville Weekly Observer,* April 13, 1837.
18. *Daily Picayune,* September 9, 1838, September 16, 1841.
19. *Daily Picayune,* September 15, 1842.
20. *Daily Picayune,* October 12, 1842.

21. *Daily Picayune,* March 21, 1844.
22. John Kendall, *History of New Orleans* (Chicago: Lewis Publishing Co., 1922).
23. *Commercial Bulletin,* September 27, 1839.
24. Succession of James M. Grice, Book E, March 24, 1844, Concordia Parish Probate Records.
25. Virginia Meacham Gould, *Chained to the Rock of Adversity: To Be Free, Black, and Female in the Old South* (Athens: University of Georgia Press, 1998), 26–28.
26. *Daily Picayune,* May 3, 1855.
27. Records of the Bureau of the Census, Record Group Number: 29, Series Number: M653, Residence Date: 1860, Home in 1860: New Orleans Ward 3, Orleans, Louisiana; Roll: M653_417, Page: 464, Family History Library Film: 803417.
28. Schafer, *Becoming Free,* 85–87.
29. Register of Free People of Color entitled to remain in the state, 1840–1864, vol. 3, page 375, NOPL.
30. Birth record for Robert Alfred Grice Thomasson, August 26, 1859, Orleans Parish Births, vol. 23, p. 302, LSA.

3. All the Social Qualities of a Gentleman: Alice Thomasson Grice

1. *Daily Picayune,* April 28, 1871.
2. Death record for Charlotte Mary Grice, age 17 months, June 20, 1865, Orleans Parish Deaths, vol. 30, p. 79, Louisiana State Archives.
3. New Orleans City Directories, 1870, 1871, 1875.
4. Charles E. Nolan, *Splendors of Faith: New Orleans Catholic Churches, 1727–1930* (Baton Rouge: Louisiana State University Press, 2010); *Daily Picayune,* March 3, 1872; *New Orleans Bulletin,* March 18, 1875.
5. John E. Rybolt, "American Vincentians in 1877–1878: The Maller Visitation Report (2)," *Vincentian Heritage Journal* 19, no. 2 (Fall 1998).
6. Huber, "Heyday of the Floating Palace"; Thomas P. Leathers Family Papers, Mss 1548, Louisiana and Lower Mississippi Valley Collections, LSU Libraries, Baton Rouge, Louisiana.
7. "Confederate Papers Relating to Citizens or Business Firms, 1861–1865." Database. Fold3.com. http://www.fold3.com : n.d. Citing NARA microfilm publication M346. Washington, D.C.: National Archives and Records Administration, 1982.
8. Ancestry.com. *U.S. IRS Tax Assessment Lists, 1862–1918* [database online]. Provo, UT, USA: Ancestry.com Operations Inc, 2008.
9. Thomas P. Leathers Family Papers, Mss 1548, Louisiana and Lower Mississippi Valley Collections, LSU Libraries, Baton Rouge, Louisiana.
10. *Daily Picayune,* September 19, 1865.
11. *Daily Picayune,* May 15, 1866.
12. *Daily Crescent,* March 13, 1868.

13. *New Orleans Commercial Bulletin*, December 21, 1869.

14. Sale of Property by William O'Brien to Alice Grice, Acts of Walter Hicks Peters, contained in the book of A. Robert, January 7, 1867, vol. 1, act 389, NARC, New Orleans.

15. *Daily Picayune*, June 15, 1866.

16. Death record for Alexander Tomasson, June 13, 1866, Orleans Parish Deaths, vol. 32, p. 439, LSA.

17. Year: 1870, Census Place: New Orleans Ward 3, Orleans, Louisiana, Roll: M593_520, Page: 518A, Family History Library Film: 552019.

18. "Louisiana, Parish Marriages, 1837–1957," database with images, *FamilySearch* (https://familysearch.org/ark:/61903/1:1:QKJW-NQZ1 : 12 March 2018), Charles Grice and Alice Thompson, 28 Apr 1871; citing Orleans, Louisiana, United States, various parish courthouses, Louisiana; FHL microfilm 907,689; Extract from Register of Marriage of St. Joseph Church, April 28, 1871, Bk. B, Vol. 4, p. 50, AANO.

19. Virginia Dominguez, *White by Definition: Social Classification in Creole Louisiana* (New Brunswick, NJ: Rutgers University Press, 1986), 26.

20. *Vicksburg Daily Commercial*, October 1, 1877.

21. *Daily Picayune*, June 25, 1870, July 16, 1870; *New Orleans Commercial Bulletin*, September 2, 1871; *Daily Picayune*, May 30, 1873; *New Orleans Republican*, September 6, 1873.

22. Baptismal Records for St. Joseph Church, March 1873, Bk. 4, p. 141, AANO.

23. *New Orleans Bulletin*, August 8, 1874.

24. Baptismal Records for St. Joseph Church, May 8, 1876, Bk. 4, p. 442, AANO.

25. Death record for Emma Maude Grice, August 1, 1876, Orleans Parish Deaths, vol. 66, p. 814, LSA.

26. Baptismal Records for St. Joseph Church, September 25, 1878, Bk. 5, AANO.

27. *School Student Lists*. Worcester, Massachusetts: American Antiquarian Society; Year: 1870, Census Place: New Orleans Ward 3, Orleans, Louisiana, Roll: M593_520, Page: 517B, Family History Library Film: 552019; Charles Vincent, "Aspects of the Family and Public Life of Antoine Dubuclet: Louisiana's Black State Treasurer, 1868–1878," *Journal of Negro History* 66, no. 1 (Spring 1981).

28. *Vicksburg Daily Commercial*, January 7, 1879.

29. *Daily Picayune*, November 18, 1884.

30. *Vicksburg Daily Commercial*, February 28, 1879.

31. *Daily Picayune*, March 10, 1879.

32. *Vicksburg Daily Commercial*, May 23, 1879.

33. See 1880 census.

34. Sale of Property by Alice Grice to New Orleans Credit Foncier Association, Acts of Edmund A. Peyroux, August 26, 1879, vol. 3, act 138, NARC, New Orleans; Sale of Property by New Orleans Credit Foncier Association to Alice Grice, Acts of Edmund A. Peyroux, September 2, 1879, vol. 3, act 144, NARC, New Orleans.

35. Year: 1900, Census Place: New Orleans Ward 3, Orleans, Louisiana, Page: 8, Enumer-

ation District: 0031, FHL microfilm: 1240571; Death record for Effie M. Grice, June 13, 1911, Orleans Parish Deaths, vol. 152, p. 520, LSA.

36. *Daily Picayune,* April 6, 1883.

37. Death record for Alice Grice, April 5, 1883, Orleans Parish Deaths, vol. 82, p. 575, LSA.

38. Year: 1860, Census Place: Algiers, Orleans, Louisiana, Roll: M653_415, Page: 1044, Family History Library Film: 803415; Year: 1870, Census Place: New Orleans Ward 14, Orleans, Louisiana, Roll: M593_525, Page: 802B, Family History Library Film: 552024; Year: 1880, Census Place: New Orleans, Orleans, Louisiana, Roll: 459, Page: 528D, Enumeration District: 023.

39. Year: 1880, Census Place: New Orleans, Orleans, Louisiana, Roll: 459, Page: 515B, Enumeration District: 023; Year: 1900, Census Place: New Orleans Ward 3, Orleans, Louisiana, Page: 8, Enumeration District: 0031, FHL microfilm: 1240571.

40. Birth record of Robert Alfred Grice Thomasson, August 26, 1859, Orleans Parish Births, vol. 23, p. 302, LSA.

41. Birth record of Bertha Grice, February 17, 1862, Orleans Parish Births, vol. 30, p. 143, LSA.

42. Birth record of Joseph Grice, November 23, 1868, Orleans Parish Births, vol. 64, p. 855, LSA; Birth record of Alice Grice, February 19, 1873, Orleans Parish Births, vol. 64, p. 855, LSA; Birth records of Angela and Emma Grice, February 24, 1876, Orleans Parish Births, vol. 69, p. 345, LSA.

43. Year: 1880, Census Place: New Orleans, Orleans, Louisiana, Roll: 459, Page: 573D, Enumeration District: 024.

44. *Daily Picayune,* November 17, 1884; Death record for Charles Grice, November 16, 1884, Orleans Parish Deaths, vol. 86, p. 204, LSA.

45. New Orleans Catholic Cemeteries Burial Records search, https://nolacatholiccemeteries.org/burial-search, accessed November 29, 2018. See 1880 census records for Grices and Grossingers; extract from Register of Marriage of St. Joseph Church, April 28, 1871, Bk. 5, p. 421, AANO.

4. A Complexion like Alabaster: Marguerite Tregre

1. *Daily Picayune,* October 4, 1850.

2. Amélie Perret Widow Joseph Paul Fabre to Guillaume Duparc, sale of slave, St. James Parish Conveyance Records, Book 15, Entry 92, p. 153.

3. New Orleans Justice of the Peace Marriage Records, vol. 4, p. 305, January 18, 1865, NOPL; Stanley Arthur Clisby, *Old Families of Louisiana* (Baltimore: Genealogical Publishing Co., 2009), 371–372.

4. Mrs. G. G. Duparc, 1854, Estate Inventories of Orleans Parish Civil Courts, Louisiana Division, NOPL.

5. Ancestry.com. *Louisiana, U.S., Compiled Marriage Index, 1718–1925* [database online]. Provo, UT, USA: Ancestry.com Operations Inc, 2004.

6. "United States Census (Slave Schedule), 1850," database with images, *FamilySearch* (https://familysearch.org/ark:/61903/1:1:HR75-29T2 : 14 March 2022), Séverin Tregre in entry for MM9.1.1/MVZJ-2HB:, 1850.

7. Maurie D. McInnis, *Slaves Waiting for Sale: Abolitionist Art and the American Slave Trade* (Chicago: University of Chicago Press, 2011), 141.

8. Edward Baptist, "'Cuffy,' 'Fancy Maids,' and 'One-Eyed Men': Rape, Commodification, and the Domestic Slave Trade in the United States," *American Historical Review* 106, no. 5 (December 2001): 1619–1650.

9. Emily A. Owens, *Consent in the Presence of Force: Sexual Violence and Black Women's Survival in Antebellum New Orleans* (Chapel Hill: University of North Carolina Press, 2023), 9; Johnson, *Soul by Soul*, 113–115.

10. McInnis, *Slaves Waiting*, 139.

11. McInnis, *Slaves Waiting*, 164.

12. John W. Blassingame, ed., *Slave Testimony: Two Centuries of Letters, Speeches, Interviews, and Autobiographies* (Baton Rouge: Louisiana State University Press, 1977), 432–437.

13. David C. Rankin, *Diary of a Christian Soldier: Rufus Kinsley and the Civil War* (New York: Cambridge University Press, 2004), 102–103.

14. Lawrence VanAlstyne, *Diary of an Enlisted Man* (New Haven, CT: Tuttle, Morehouse, & Taylor Co., 1910), 199.

15. Lynette Ater Taynner, ed., *Chained to the Land: Voices from Cotton and Cane Plantations* (Durham, NC: John F. Butler Publisher, 2014), 202.

16. Harmeet Kaur, "A New DNA Study Offers Insight into the Horror-Story of the Trans-Atlantic Slave Trade," *CNN*, July 26, 2020, https://www.cnn.com/2020/07/26/us/dna-transatlantic-slave-trade-study-scn-trnd/index.html; Owens, *Consent in the Presence of Force*, 14.

17. *Daily Picayune*, November 13, 1844.

18. Auguste Dufau to Auguste Pajaud, Sale of Slave, Acts of Notary Philipe Pedesclaux, January 25, 1822, vol. 23, act 78, NARC; Pajaud to Raymond Locoul, Sale of Slave, Acts of Notary Hugues Lavergne, February 2, 1824, vol. 13, act 2245, NARC.

19. *Courrier de la Louisiane*, March 12, 1824.

20. Raymond Locoul Anne Prudhomme Widow Duparc, Sale of Slave, Acts of Notary Hugues Lavergne, May 21, 1826, vol. 18, act 3545, NARC.

21. Succession of Louis Demessiere Duparc, opened April 21, 1852, docket no. 4358, Third District Court of New Orleans, NOPL.

22. Will of Guillaume Duparc, probated July 30, 1863, Orleans Parish Will Book Vol. 13, 1863–1865, p. 23.

23. Claim No. 695, Elise Lecoul.

24. Weaver, *Thank God My Regiment*, 100.

25. Claim No. 695, Elise Lecoul.

26. Weaver, *Thank God My Regiment*, 75, xix, 88, 91, 100.

27. Owens, *Consent in the Presence of Force*, 11; Weaver, *Thank God My Regiment*, 100.

28. Weaver, *Thank God My Regiment*, 121–122.
29. Rankin, *Diary of a Christian Soldier*, 206, 50.
30. Weaver, *Thank God My Regiment*, 66.
31. Annie Jeter Carmouche Papers, Mss 2878, Louisiana and the Lower Mississippi Valley Collections, Hill Memorial Library, Louisiana State University.
32. Weaver, *Thank God My Regiment*, 149.

5. St. Margaret, Keeper of Furnished Rooms: Marguerite Tregre Grossinger

1. 1869 *Soards' New Orleans City Directory*; *Daily Picayune*, March 8, 1879.
2. Juliana Dresvina, *A Maid with a Dragon: The Cult of St Margaret of Antioch in Medieval England* (Oxford: Oxford University Press, 2016).
3. Norman Marmillion and Sand Warren Marmillion, eds., *Memories of the Old Plantation Home* (Vacherie, LA: Zoë Co., 2007), 18.
4. Death record for Guillaume Duparc, age 70, July 26, 1863, Orleans Parish Deaths, vol. 24, p. 25, LSA.
5. Sale of Lot and Buildings, Pierre Gabriel Bertrand to Romain Brugier, July 16, 1839, Acts of Theodore Seghers, vol. 32, act 598, NARC, New Orleans.
6. James S. Zacharie, *New Orleans Guide* (New Orleans: New Orleans News Co., 1885), 28.
7. *New Orleans Times*, January 29, 1867.
8. Richard Campanella, *Bourbon Street: A History* (Baton Rouge: Louisiana State University Press, 2014), p. 65.
9. Emily Clark, *The Strange History of the American Quadroon: Free Women of Color in the Revolutionary Atlantic World* (Chapel Hill: University of North Carolina Press, 2013), 171–172.
10. Grace King, *New Orleans: The Place and the People* (New York: Macmillan, 1895), 347.
11. Gould, *Chained to the Rock*, 7.
12. Eliza Potter, *A Hairdresser's Experience in High Life* (Cincinnati: Eliza Potter, 1859), 160.
13. 1870 and 1871 *Soards' New Orleans City Directories*.
14. *The Daily Nashville Union*, August 14, 1851.
15. *The Daily Picayune*, September 1, 1851.
16. *The Daily Nashville Union*, August 14, 1851.
17. *The Daily Picayune*, July 3, 1858; *The New Orleans Crescent*, July 28, 1858.
18. *The Daily Delta*, November 13, 1860; *The New Orleans Crescent*, May 6, 1861.
19. Year: 1870, Census Place: Middletown, Monmouth, New Jersey, Roll: M593_875, Page: 287A; Sarah Grossinger, administrator of Charles Grossinger deceased, *Administrators Bonds, 1861–1886, Vol C, 181*; New Jersey Surrogate's Court (Monmouth County).
20. *The Daily Nashville Union*, August 14, 1851.
21. Year: 1880, Census Place: New Orleans, Orleans, Louisiana, Roll: 459, Page: 515B, Enumeration District: 023.

22. Claim No. 695, Elise Lecoul.

23. Elisha Robinson and Roger H. Pidgeon, *Robinson's Atlas of the City of New Orleans, Louisiana* (New York: E. Robinson, 1883), plate 5.

24. Succession of Anais Rivarde Hopkins, opened July 16, 1896, docket no. 50360, Civil District Court, NOPL; History of Music Project, *Celebrities in El Dorado 1850–1906*, Volume 4 (Northern California: Work Projects Administration, 1939), 126; *New York Times*, November 18, 1895; "Achille Rivarde," *The Musical Courier* 31, no. 12 (September 28, 1895): 8.

25. New Orleans Justice of the Peace Marriage Records, Vol. 4, p. 305, January 18, 1865, Louisiana Division, New Orleans Public Library; Compiled service record, Justin Stewart, Sgt, Company K, 84th US Colored Infantry, Carded Records Showing Military Service of Soldiers Who Fought in Volunteer Organizations During the American Civil War, compiled 1890–1912, documenting the period 1861–1866, record group 94, National Archives, Washington, D.C; Year: 1880, Census Place: 7th Ward, St. James Parish, Louisiana, Roll: 468, Family History Film: 1254468, Page: 619D, Enumeration District: 159, Image: 0490.

26. Death record for Armantine Stewart, April 23, 1887, Orleans Parish Deaths, vol. 91, p. 9, LSA. [Age is misreported; she was actually 62.]; Cypress Grove Cemetery Interments, Volume 3, April 24, 1887, NOPL.

27. *The Daily Picayune*, July 10, 1847.

28. Extract from Register of Marriage of St. Joseph Church, April 28, 1871, Bk. 5, p. 421, AANO.

29. Virginia R. Dominguez, *White by Definition* (New Brunswick, NJ: Rutgers University Press, 1997), 28–29, 57; *The Times-Democrat*, June 28, 1894; *Daily Picayune*, July 30, 1894.

6. Tears in the Telling: Georgina Lombard Gaal

1. Alexander Gaal (Captain, Co. F, 1st Florida Cavalry, Civil War), pension application no. 952104, certificate no. 825919, Case Files of Approved Pension Applications, 1861–1934, Civil War and Later Pension Files, Department of Veterans Affairs, Record Group 15, NARA.

2. Alexander Gaal Pension.

3. Nathalie Dessens, *From Saint-Domingue to New Orleans: Migration and Influences* (Gainesville: University of Florida Press).

4. C. F. Arrowood, "The Journal of Captain Isaac L. Baker," *Southwestern Historical Quarterly* 30, no. 4 (April 1927): 274.

5. Baptism of Marie Almaide, daughter of Magdeleine Dupuy, August 10, 1817, (SLC, B 29, 161), AANO.

6. Marriage of Noel Gaspard Dupuy and Marie Marcelite Durocher, March 23, 1818, (SLC, M6, 209), AANO.

7. Sale of Property from Marie Bodaille free woman of color to Magdelaine Dupuy free woman of color, Acts of Carlos Pollock, December 15, 1819, vol. 4, act 185, NARC, New Orleans.

8. Alexander Gaal Pension; Passenger Lists of Vessels Arriving at New Orleans, Louisiana, 1820–1902, NAI Number: 2824927, Record Group Title: Records of the Immigration and Naturalization Service, Record Group Number: 85, NARA.

9. Death Record for Leonard Lombard, age 35, July 15, 1845, Orleans Parish Deaths, vol. 9, p. 799, LSA.

10. Ronnie W. Clayton, *Mother Wit: The Ex-Slave Narratives of the Louisiana Writers' Project* (Lawrence: University of Kansas Press, 1990), 74.

11. Bell, *Revolution*, 37, 38.

12. Emily Clark, *Masterless Mistresses: The New Orleans Ursulines and the Development of a New World Society, 1727–1834* (Chapel Hill: The University of North Carolina Press, 2007), 168; Melissa Daggett, *Spiritualism in Nineteenth-Century New Orleans: The Life and Times of Henry Louis Rey* (Oxford: University of Mississippi Press, 2016), 89.

13. Val Alstyne, 158.

14. Myers, *Forging Freedom*, 83, 121; Will of Marie Magdeleine Dupuy, fwc, probated September 9, 1848, Orleans Parish Will Book Vol. 8, 1844–1855, p. 402.

15. Records of the Bureau of the Census, Record Group Number: 29, Series Number: M432, Residence Date: 1850, Home in 1850: New Orleans Municipality 1 Ward 4, Orleans, Louisiana, Roll: 235, Page: 167b.

16. *The Daily Picayune*, November 29, 1913.

17. 1868 *Soards' New Orleans City Directories*.

18. *Daily Picayune*, October 4, 1850.

19. Records of the Bureau of the Census, Record Group Number: 29, Series Number: M653, Residence Date: 1860, Home in 1860: New Orleans Ward 5, Orleans, Louisiana, Roll: M653_418, Page: 665, Family History Library Film: 803418; Birth record for Marie Heno, January 19, 1850, Orleans Parish Births, vol. 10, p. 296, LSA; Birth record for Paul Heno, March 8, 1852, Orleans Parish Births, vol. 10, p. 462, LSA.

20. 1868 *Soards' New Orleans City Directories;* Seventh Census of the United States, 1850, Record Group: Records of the Bureau of the Census; Record Group Number: 29, NARA Microform Publication: M432; Sale of a Slave from Almaide Heno fwc to Robert Joseph Ker, Acts of Amedée Ductel, February 3, 1860, vol. 81, act 44, NARC, New Orleans.

21. Gould, *Chained to the Rock*, 28.

22. Schafer, *Slavery, the Civil Law*, 199.

23. Mortgage for Marie A. Heno from Monplaisir Fleury, Acts of Hugues Pedesclaux, June 24, 1858, vol. 23, act 102, NARC, New Orleans; Eighth Census of the United States 1860, Series Number: M653, Record Group: Records of the Bureau of the Census, Record Group Number: 29; Marie Almaide Heno to Dauphine Chauvet, Widow Alexandre Raymond François, lot in Tremé, March 22, 1870, C.O.B. Book 86, Folio 707, NARC, New Orleans; Almaide Heno purchased the property from Martin Halbritter on September 7, 1864. See indices of notary Abel Dreyfous; Birth record for Marie Alline Dupuy, December 1, 1864, Orleans Parish Births, vol. 30, p. 541, LSA; Birth record for Marie Dupuy, January 12, 1870,

Orleans Parish Births, vol. 53, p. 277, LSA; Alexander Gaal Pension; Year: 1870, Census Place: New Orleans Ward 5, Orleans, Louisiana, Roll: M593_521, Page: 121A.

24. Ancestry.com. *U.S., Freedmen's Bureau Records, 1865–1878* [database on-line]. Lehi, UT, USA: Ancestry.com Operations, Inc., 2021; Now Armstrong Park, this was St. Ann, corner of Villere and Marais, now the 1400 block of St. Ann, Square #168. The New Orleans Notarial Archives could not trace it, but Property Management at New Orleans City Hall might be able to locate it.

25. Year: 1880, Census Place: New Orleans, Orleans, Louisiana, Roll: 459, Page: 399D, Enumeration District: 019; Eugene Pivany, *Hungarians in the American Civil War* (Cleveland: Dongo, 1913), 35.

26. Alexander Gaal Pension.

27. Alexander Gaal Pension.

28. Alexander Gaal Pension.

29. "Louisiana Parish Marriages, 1837–1957," database with images, *FamilySearch* (https://familysearch.org/ark:/61903/1:1:QKJ4-5Y98 : 17 February 2021), Erwin Hanmer and Aline Dupuy, 23 Feb 1892; citing Orleans, Louisiana, United States, various parish courthouses, Louisiana; FHL microfilm 907,788; Birth record for Wendell Hanmer, April 8, 1893, Orleans Parish Births, vol. 97, p. 458, LSA; Birth record for Juanita Hanmer, February 10, 1895, Orleans Parish Births, vol. 104, p. 192, LSA; Birth record for Erwin Roy Hanmer, November 27, 1896, Orleans Parish Births, vol. 108, p. 489, LSA; Birth record for Hazel Hanmer, November 22, 1897, Orleans Parish Births, vol. 112, illegible, LSA; Death Record for Juanita Hammer, July 11, 1895, Orleans Parish Deaths, vol. 109, p. 144, LSA; Death Record for Aline Dupuy, February 20, 1898, Orleans Parish Deaths, vol. 115, p. 988, LSA; New York State Archives, Albany, New York, State Population Census Schedules, 1915, Election District: 21, Assembly District: 02, City: New York, County: Kings, Page: 59; Year: 1930, Census Place: Queens, Queens, New York, Page: 17A, Enumeration District: 0243, FHL microfilm: 2341328; Year: 1940, Census Place: Trenton, Wayne, Michigan, Roll: m-t0627–01834, Page: 4B, Enumeration District: 82–183C.

30. David M. Roth, "Louisiana Hurricane History" (PDF), *National Weather Service*, 2009.

31. Year: 1900, Census Place: New Orleans Ward 5, Orleans, Louisiana, Roll: 571, Page: 1; Enumeration District: 0045; Year: 1910, Census Place: New Orleans Ward 5, Orleans, Louisiana, Roll: T624_521, Page: 2b, Enumeration District: 0074, FHL microfilm: 1374534.

32. Alexander Gaal Pension; *The St. Bernard Voice*, March 9, 1912; *Daily Picayune*, December 9, 1912.

33. Alexander Gaal Pension.

34. Alexander Gaal Pension.

35. Death Record for Georgina Lombard Gaal, October 5, 1917, Orleans Parish Deaths, vol. 170, p. 308, LSA.

36. Alexander Gaal Pension.

7. Scratch the Surface: Marie Heno Forstall

1. Year: 1880, Census Place: New Orleans, Orleans, Louisiana, Roll: 461, Page: 173D, Enumeration District: 034.
2. 1891 *Soards' New Orleans City Directories*; 1902 *Soards' New Orleans City Directories*.
3. *Daily Picayune*, January 20, 1886.
4. Charles Gayarré, *The Creoles of History and the Creoles of Romance* (New Orleans: C. E. Hopkins, 1885); Sybil Kein, ed., *Creole: The History and Legacy of Louisiana's Free People of Color* (Baton Rouge: Louisiana State University Press, 200), 131; Alcée Fortier, *A Few Words about the Creoles of Louisiana: An Address Delivered at the Ninth Annual Convention of the Louisiana Educational Association* (Baton Rouge: Truth Book and Job Office, 1892); *Daily Picayune*, February 8, 1886.
5. Gayarré, *Creoles of History*.
6. Baptism of Carlos Hartur Nicolas Gayarré, May 5, 1826, (SLC, B 36, 158), AANO.
7. Marcus Christian Collection, Mss 11, Earl K. Long Library, University of New Orleans.
8. Marie Magdelaine Dupuy Will, Acts of Adolphe Mazureau, May 11, 1848, vol. 34, act 215, NARC, New Orleans.
9. *Miles Register*, November 5, 1825.
10. Virginia Meacham Gould and Charles E. Nolan, eds., *No Cross, No Crown: Black Nuns in Nineteenth Century New Orleans* (Bloomington: Indiana University Press, 2001), xxvii; Natasha L. McPherson, "'There was a Tradition Among the Women': New Orleans's Colored Creole Women and the Making of a Community in the Tremé and Seventh Ward, 1791–1930" (PhD diss., Emory University, 2011), 7, 8.
11. Stuart O. Landry Jr., ed., *Voyage to Louisiana by C. C. Robin 1803–1805, an Abridged Translation from the Original French* (Gretna, LA: Pelican Publishing, 1966); Samuel Wilson Jr., ed., *Southern Travels: Journal of John H. B. Latrobe, 1834* (New Orleans: Historic New Orleans Collection, 1986), 49.
12. Wilson, *Southern Travels*, 77.
13. Bell, *Revolution*, 112; Clark, *Strange History of the American Quadroon*, 148–159; Wilson, *Southern Travels*, 79.
14. *Louisiana Gazette*, September 22, 1810.
15. *Louisiana Gazette*, September 22, 1810.
16. Alecia Long, *Great Southern Babylon: Sex, Race, and Respectability in New Orleans, 1865–1920* (Baton Rouge: Louisiana State University Press, 2004); Emily Clark, *Strange History of the American Quadroon*; Kenneth Aslakson, "The 'Quadroon-Plaçage' Myth of Antebellum New Orleans: Anglo-American (Mis)interpretations of a French-Caribbean Phenomenon," *Journal of Social History* 45, no. 3 (Spring 2012): 709–734; McPherson, "'There Was a Tradition,'" 12.
17. Clayton, *Mother Wit*, 73, 81.
18. Gould, *No Cross, No Crown*, 63, 73; McPherson, "'There Was a Tradition,'" 11–13, 29–30.

19. Potter, *A Hairdresser's Experience*, 190.

20. King, *New Orleans*, 347–348.

21. Year: 1900, Census Place: New Orleans Ward 5, Orleans, Louisiana, Roll: 571, Page: 14, Enumeration District: 0046; Grace King, *Creole Families of New Orleans* (Baton Rouge: Claitor's Publishing Division, 1971), 357–367.

22. Records of the Bureau of the Census, Record Group Number: 29, Series Number: M653, Residence Date: 1860, Home in 1860: New Orleans Ward 6, Orleans, Louisiana, Roll: M653_419, Page: 60, Family History Library Film: 803419; *Times-Democrat*, November 6, 1892; King, *Creole Families*, 357–367.

23. *L'Abeille*, December 19, 1864.

24. Year: 1870, Census Place: New Orleans Ward 6, Orleans, Louisiana, Roll: M593_522, Page: 318A; Birth record for Josephine Jeanne Forstall, June 5, 1881, Orleans Parish Births, vol. 77, p. 385, LSA; Birth record for Willie Forstall, September 2, 1882, Orleans Parish Births, vol. 96, p. 647, LSA; Birth record for Lucie Forstall, February 8, 1884, Orleans Parish Births, vol. 96, p. 648, LSA; Birth record for George Forstall, March 10, 1886, Orleans Parish Births, vol. 96, p. 648, LSA; *The Daily Picayune*, January 30, 1886.

25. "Louisiana Parish Marriages, 1837–1957," database with images, *FamilySearch* (https://familysearch.org/ark:/61903/1:1:QKJW-RN2T : 17 February 2021), William Forstall and Marie Héno, 08 Jul 1889; citing Orleans, Louisiana, United States, various parish courthouses, Louisiana; FHL microfilm 907,700; *L'Abeille*, February 7, 1884; *Daily Picayune*, January 30, 1886; *L'Abeille*, April 1, 1876; *Daily Picayune*, September 13, 1878; 1890 *Soards' New Orleans City Directories*; Gould, *No Cross, No Crown*, 18.

26. "Louisiana Parish Marriages, 1837–1957," database with images, *FamilySearch* (https://familysearch.org/ark:/61903/1:1:QKJW-RN2T : 17 February 2021), William Forstall and Marie Héno, 08 Jul 1889; citing Orleans, Louisiana, United States, various parish courthouses, Louisiana; FHL microfilm 907,700; Michael Eugene Crutcher, *Tremé: Race and Place in a New Orleans Neighborhood* (Athens: University of Georgia Press, 2010), 30.

27. Death Record for William Forstall, May 20, 1895, Orleans Parish Deaths, vol. 108, p. 795, LSA; 1895 *Soards' New Orleans City Directories*; Year: 1900, Census Place: New Orleans Ward 5, Orleans, Louisiana; Roll: 571; Page: 14, Enumeration District: 0046.

28. 1901 *Soards' New Orleans City Directory*; 1903 *Soards' New Orleans City Directory*; *Daily Picayune*, February 2, 1896; 1905 *Soards' New Orleans City Directory*; 1907 *Soards' New Orleans City Directory*; *Times-Democrat*, June 14, 1908.

8. An Upright, Honorable Existence: Marguerite Tregre Grossinger and the Grice Children

1. Death record for Effie M. Grice, June 13, 1911, Orleans Parish Deaths, vol. 152, p. 520, LSA.
2. Succession of Effie Grice, #97684, filed March 24, 1913, Orleans Parish.
3. Effie Grice Will, May 25, 1911, Will Book Vol. 15–16, Civil District Court, Orleans Parish.
4. Succession of Effie Grice, #97684.

5. Charles Grice Embezzlement Trial, #23933 B and #24338 B, Louisiana Criminal District Court (Orleans Parish).

6. *New Orleans Item,* September 22, 1903.

7. Carolina Abboud, "William Stewart Halsted (1852–1922)," *Embryo Project Encyclopedia* (July 23, 2017).

8. *Daily Picayune,* December 15, 1889.

9. Death record for Maggie Grossinger, age 49 years, April 20, 1898, Orleans Parish Deaths, vol. 116, p. 321, Louisiana State Archives.

10. Cypress Grove Cemetery #2 Interments 1863–1929, v. 3, April 21, 1898, City Archives, Louisiana Division, New Orleans Public Library.

11. Year: 1900, Census Place: New Orleans Ward 3, Orleans, Louisiana, Page: 8, Enumeration District: 0031, FHL microfilm: 1240571.

12. Greenwood Cemetery Lot Cards, City Archives, Louisiana Division, New Orleans Public Library; Greenwood and Cypress Grove Cemeteries, Interments, v. 2, August 11, 1905, v. 2, August 18, 1905, v. 3, June 14, 1911, City Archives, Louisiana Division, New Orleans Public Library; Archdiocese of New Orleans, Department of the Archives, St. Joseph's Funerals Volume 1, August 18, 1905.

13. *New Orleans Item,* February 1, 1906; *New Orleans Item,* March 5, 1916.

14. Douglas C. M. Slawson, "Segregated Catholicism: The Origins of Saint Katharine's Parish, New Orleans," *Vincentian Heritage Journal* 17, no. 3 (1996).

15. Death record for Millie Thompson, August 30, 1867, Orleans Parish Deaths, vol. 39, p. 17, LSA.

16. Marcia Alesan Dawkins, *Clearly Invisible: Racial Passing and the Color of Cultural Identity* (Waco, TX: Baylor University Press, 2014), 57–59.

17. Dawkins, *Clearly Invisible,* 59–60.

18. Dawkins, *Clearly Invisible,* 61, 62.

19. Joel Williamson, *New People: Miscegenation and Mulattoes in the United States* (New York: Free Press, 1996).

20. Elaine K. Ginsberg, *Passing and the Fictions of Identity* (Durham, NC: Duke University Press, 1996); Williamson, *New People,* 98; Sherita L Johnson, "Passing," *The American Mosaic: The African American Experience,* ABC-CLIO, 2016. Web. 28 Apr. 2016.

21. *New Orleans Item,* September 5, 1912; Death record for Adolph Bonée, September 5, 1912, Orleans Parish Deaths, vol. 155, p. 891, LSA.

22. Greenwood Cemetery database of burials, accessed December 1, 2018, http://fcbacms.greenwoodnola.com/publicSearch.aspx?lname=Grice&fname=&mname=; *New Orleans Item,* July 13, 1913.

9. A Menace to the Purity of the White Race: Marie Heno Forstall

1. *New Orleans Item,* July 13, 1913; Marcus Christian Collection, Mss 11, Earl K. Long Library, University of New Orleans.

2. *St. Landry Clarion,* July 25, 1908.

3. *New Orleans Item,* June 2, 1909; *Daily Picayune,* September 14, 1909; *Daily Picayune,* April 29, 1912.

4. *New Orleans Item,* March 17, 1910.

5. *Daily Picayune,* November 18, 1909.

6. *Daily Picayune,* November 18, 1909.

7. *New Orleans Item,* November 30, 1909.

8. *New Orleans Item,* April 29, 1910.

9. *Duvigneaud v. Loquet et al.,* #19314, October 21, 1912, Supreme Court of Louisiana.

10. Succession of Fortier, #13094, April 3, 1899, Supreme Court of Louisiana.

11. Michelle Brittain, "Miscegenation and Competing Definitions of Race in Twentieth-Century Louisiana," *Journal of Southern History* 71, no. 3 (August 2005).

12. R. G. Dun & Co Credit, Louisiana Volume 10, p. 358; *L'Abeille,* November 11, 1871; Alcée Fortier, ed., *Louisiana: Comprising Sketches of Parishes, Towns, Events, Institutions, and Persons, Vol. 1* (Madison, WI: Century Historical Association, 1914), 425; Marriage of Henriette Feraud and Adolphe Lanauze, November 25, 1851, St. Mary Church, Volume 5, page 346, AANO; Cyprian Davis, *Henriette Delille: Servant of Slaves, Witness to the Poor* (New Orleans: Archdiocese of New Orleans, 2004); Funeral of Elizabeth Wiltz, natural daughter of the late Jean Baptiste Wiltz, November 26, 1837, St. Louis Cathedral Funeral Records, Volume 9, Part II, AANO; Funeral of Anne Poeyfarre, natural daughter of the late Jean Baptiste Wiltz, May 9, 1838, St. Louis Cathedral Funeral Records, Volume 9, Part II, AANO.

13. *Times-Picayune,* April 12, 1936.

14. *Times-Picayune,* June 14, 1936; *Times-Picayune,* April 1, 1915.

15. *Daily Picayune,* July 13, 1913; *Brookhaven Semi-Weekly Leader,* July 19, 1913.

16. *New Orleans Item,* July 13, 1913.

17. *Times-Democrat,* July 13, 1913; *New Orleans Item,* July 13, 1913; Walter Johnson, "The Slave Trader, the White Slave, and the Politics of Racial Determination," *Journal of American History* 87 (2000): 27, 34.

10. Tearing Down the Bars: Marie Heno Forstall

1. *New Orleans Item,* July 14, 1913.

2. *Daily Picayune,* June 30, 1900; *Daily Picayune,* June 15, 1913; *Daily Picayune,* July 6, 1913.

3. Arthé A. Anthony "'Lost Boundaries': Racial Passing and Poverty in Segregated New Orleans," *Louisiana History* 36, no. 3 (Summer 1995): 298, 306.

4. Anthony, "'Lost Boundaries,'" 297, 304.

5. *New Orleans Item,* July 15, 1913; *New Orleans Item,* August 20, 1913; *Daily Picayune,* August 20, 1913; *Daily Picayune,* November 29, 1913.

6. *Marie Forstall, Widow of William Forstall v. City Board of Health,* No. 106603, December 8, 1913, Civil District Court, Division D, Orleans Parish; *Daily Picayune,* February 3, 1914; *New Orleans Item,* March 3, 1914.

7. *Daily Picayune*, February 4, 1914.

8. Death record for Paul Henry Lanauze, June 27, 1940, Orleans Parish Deaths, vol. 214, p. 1506, LSA; *Times-Picayune*, April 12, 1836.

9. Year: 1930, Census Place: New Orleans, Orleans, Louisiana, Page: 19A, Enumeration District: 0052, FHL microfilm: 2340537; Seventeenth Census of the United States, Year: 1950; Census Place: New Orleans, Orleans, Louisiana; Roll: 5279; Page: 4; Enumeration District: 36–138; Death record for Marie Dupuy Forstall, December 8, 1919, Orleans Parish Deaths, vol. 177, p. 915, LSA.

10. *Times-Picayune*, February 18, 1947; *Naomi Drake v. Department of Health*, City of New Orleans Civil Service Commission, Appel 391, in Civil Service Department Minutes, Classified City Employees, 1965, microfilm AI 300, roll #66–155 (NOPL).

11. *State ex rel. Eugene Lewis [sic] Heno v. Naomi M. Drake*, 176 So. 2d 226 (La. Ct. App. 1965).

12. *Heirs of J. B. Heno v. E. S. Dufossat*, #11911, Civil District Court, Orleans Parish; *George Heno, Solidelle Heno, and Marguerite Heno v. Pierre Heno*, 9 Mart. (O.S.) 643 (1821) docket no. 510, SCLHA, UNO; Mary Williams, "Private Lives, Public Orders: The Heno Family and the Legal Regulation of Sexuality in Early National Louisiana," paper presented at the Berkshire Conference on the History of Women, University of Connecticut, June 2002; Jennifer M. Spear, *Race, Sex and Social Order in Early New Orleans* (Baltimore: Johns Hopkins University Press, 2009), 203–204.

13. Records of the Bureau of the Census, Record Group Number: 29, Series Number: M432, Residence Date: 1850, Home in 1850: New Orleans Municipality 1 Ward 7, Orleans, Louisiana, Roll: 236, Page: 384b; *Daily Picayune*, September 8, 1860; Birth record for Paul Heno, March 8, 1852, Orleans Parish Births, vol. 10, p. 462, LSA; Birth record for Marie Madeleine Aline Heno, April 11, 1855, Orleans Parish Births, vol. 10, p. 695, LSA; "Louisiana Parish Marriages, 1837–1957," *FamilySearch* (https://www.familysearch.org/ark:/61903/1:1:QK JC-CM17 : Mon Oct 23 15:30:00 UTC 2023), Entry for Eugene Heno and Adolph Heno, 21 Mar 1910.

14. *Naomi Drake v. Department of Health*, City of New Orleans Civil Service Commission, Appel 391, in Civil Service Department Minutes, Classified City Employees, 1965, microfilm AI 300, roll #66–155 (NOPL).

15. *Naomi Drake v. Department of Health*, City of New Orleans Civil Service Commission.

16. Dominguez, *White by Definition*, 159.

17. *Times-Picayune*, September 5, 1993.

18. *Times-Picayune*, June 18, 1922; "Alma Forstall Studio Teaches How to Dance," *Times-Picayune*, January 12, 1930. See notes on Hanmers in chapter 6; *Birmingham News*, March 20, 1929; *Times-Picayune*, September 5, 1993.

19. Receipt for $150 for a plot in Greenwood Cemetery, Tulane University Special Collections Facebook Page, posted June 18, 2018, accessed, June 18, 2018, https://www.facebook.com/tuspecialcollections/photos/a.209842095709170/2190357454324281; *Times-Picayune*, January 11, 1967.

Epilogue

1. Francis E. Dumas Pension.
2. 1901 *Soards' New Orleans City Directories*.
3. James G. Hollandsworth Jr., *The Louisiana Native Guards: The Black Military Experience during the Civil War* (Baton Rouge: Louisiana State University Press, 1998), 46–47; Shirley Elizabeth Thompson, *Exiles at Home: The Struggle to Become American in Creole New Orleans* (Cambridge, MA: Harvard University Press, 2009), 162; Hollandsworth, *Louisiana Native Guards*, 74.
4. Hollandsworth, *Louisiana Native Guards*, 110–111.
5. Justin A. Nystrom, *New Orleans after the Civil War: Race, Politics, and a New Birth of Freedom* (Baltimore: Johns Hopkins University Press, 2010), 20, 186; Hollandsworth, *Louisiana Native Guards*, 110.
6. Michael A. Ross, *The Great New Orleans Kidnapping Case: Race, Law, and Justice in the Reconstruction Era* (New York: Oxford University Press), 27, 37, 215–219.
7. Sister Dorothea Olga McCants, ed., *Our People and Our History: Fifty Creole Portraits by Rodolphe Lucien Desdunes* (Baton Rouge: Louisiana State University Press, 1973), 92–94, 140–141.
8. *New York Times*, May 16, 1893.
9. Year: 1900, Census Place: New Orleans Ward 11, Orleans, Louisiana, Roll: 574, Page: 26, Enumeration District: 0112; Year: 1910, Census Place: New Orleans Ward 12, Orleans, Louisiana, Roll: T624_524, Page: 5a, Enumeration District: 0193, FHL microfilm: 1374537.
10. Francis E. Dumas Pension.
11. *New Orleans States-Item*, June 14, 1978, June 15, 1978; *Times-Picayune*, June 15, 1978; *New York Times*, July 6, 1983.
12. Hollandsworth, *Louisiana Native Guards*, 26.
13. Hobbs, *A Chosen Exile*, 31.
14. Dominguez, *White by Definition*, 161.

INDEX

Adams, St. Clair, 128, 130
Anthony, Arthé A., 141
Anti-Miscegenation Law, 81, 126, 127, 135, 148, 151

balls, 101–6
Battle of Liberty Place, 133
Battle of New Orleans, 84
Bechet, Marie Philomene, 128, 131
Becnel, Magdelaine Haydel, 22, 23
Becnel, Michel, 25, 28
Bellau, Marie Louise, 147
Board of Health (New Orleans), 115–16, 118, 123, 125, 132, 134, 135, 141–45, 147, 148
Bonee, Adolph, 123
branding of enslaved, 67
Brugier, Romain, 75
Bureau of Pensions, 94–96
Butler, General Benjamin, 25, 26

Cable, George Washington, 99, 100
Cambre, Marie Baselite, 4–7
Carr, Odile, 74
caste system, 8, 9, 14–16, 53, 65, 78, 89, 99, 107, 118, 122, 129, 130, 132, 141, 148, 150, 153, 155, 156
Charbonnet, Lloys, 130, 138, 141, 142

Charles, Robert, 139
Charleston, SC, xi, 1
Chretien, Judge Frank D., 130
Christian, Marcus, 21, 100, 125
Civil Service Commission (New Orleans), 148
Civil War, 7, 15–17, 20, 25, 26, 46–49, 54, 65, 68–74, 77, 79, 90–92, 108, 130, 153, 155
Clark, Emily, 86, 105
coartación, 13
Code Noir, 11, 13
Comité des Citoyens, 119, 154
"concubinage," 89, 90, 101, 103, 106
Concubinage Law, 126–30, 132, 135, 138
Cook, Marie Azelie, 32, 33
Creole, xi, 1, 5, 7, 9, 12–17, 20, 27, 28, 36, 48, 53, 57, 59, 62, 63, 65, 70, 74, 78–81, 83–86, 89, 98–104, 106, 108, 109, 116–19, 122, 128, 130–32, 136, 137, 140, 141, 146, 148–50, 155
Cypress Grove Cemetery, 80, 116, 150

D. H. Holmes, 111
Daniels, Colonel Nathan, 27, 28, 68–74, 78, 79, 152
Dawkins, Marcia Alesan, 119
Delille, Henriette, 133
DNA analysis, 66

181

Dominguez, Virginia R., 148, 155
Drake, Naomi, 145–49, 154
Dreyfous Co. Ltd., 111
Dubuclet, Oscar, 54, 55
Duhé, Blaise, 4, 7
Duhé, Eli, 4, 5
Duhé, Evariste, 7
Duhé, Jacques, 4–7
Duhé, Lawrence, 7
Dumas, Elisabeth Rivarde, 24
Dumas, Francis Ernest, 25–28, 68–70, 79, 80, 152–55
Dumas, Henry, 152
Dumas, Joseph, 24–26
Duparc & Locoul Plantation, 60–63, 67, 68, 70, 74, 157
Duparc, Guillaume "Flagy," 27, 28, 60–63, 68, 70, 74, 75, 79, 81
Duparc, Nanette, 67
Duplantier, Armand, 6
Duplantier, Edwige, 6, 7
Dupuy, Charles, 90
Dupuy, Corinne, 90–96
Dupuy, Magdelaine Chevalier, 84–86
Dupuy, Noel Gaspard, 84, 85
Duvigneaud, Adelard, 128–32

Edwards, Governor Edwin, 154
Evans, Walter, 114
Evergreen Plantation, 22–26, 28, 68

Fabre, Judge Joseph, 62
Fanchon, Agathe, 146
"fancy girls," 62–67
Feraud, Henriette, 133
Fonvergne, Anita, 85, 105
Forstall, Alma, 149
Forstall, Felix, 108
Forstall, George, 109
Forstall, Heloise DeJan, 108, 110
Forstall, Jeanne, 109, 142

Forstall, Lucie, 109, 142
Forstall, Marie Heno, 83, 88, 97–101, 107, 109–12, 125, 136–44, 146, 147, 149, 154, 155
Forstall, William, Jr., 109, 11, 112, 123–26, 130, 132, 134–39, 141–44, 149
Forstall, William, Sr., 81, 93, 98, 108–10, 123
Fortier, Alcée, 132
Fortier, F. M., 132
Fortier, Jean Michel, 131
Freedmen's Bureau, 51, 90
free people of color, xi, 3, 9, 13–17, 19, 23, 25, 39, 40, 43, 44, 46, 61, 65, 76, 84, 86, 88, 89, 93, 97, 105, 106, 110, 130, 131, 133, 142, 143, 146, 147, 153
French Quarter, 23, 48, 73, 75, 78, 84, 95, 98, 103, 110, 152
"furnished rooms," 75, 76, 88, 93, 94, 100

Gaal, Alexander, 81, 83, 91–96, 110
Gaal, Georgina Lombard, 18, 83–97, 99–101, 105, 107, 109, 149, 154, 155
Gayarré, Charles, 75, 76, 99, 100, 108
Grand Isle, LA, 93, 96
Greenwood Cemetery, 113, 116, 150
Grice, Alice Olivia Comadina, 54, 57, 113, 116, 117, 123, 141, 150–152
Grice, Alice Thomasson, 18, 20, 21, 29–31, 35, 39, 42–48, 51–57, 62, 64, 81, 100, 107, 117, 118, 154, 155
Grice, Angela Clothilde, 54, 58, 114
Grice, Ann, 41–43
Grice, Bertha, 54, 57, 58, 114
Grice, Charles, 18, 29, 30, 41, 44, 46, 49, 50, 52, 53, 115, 118
Grice, Charles Francis, 54, 58, 114, 115
Grice, Effie, 56–59, 113–16, 123, 141, 150, 152
Grice, James M., 41–43
Grice, James Oscar, 54, 57, 58, 114, 123
Grice, Joseph, 54, 57, 58, 114, 115
Grice, Robert, 46, 53, 54, 56–58, 118, 123

Grossinger, Charles, 58, 59, 76–78, 81, 82, 91, 96, 110–13, 116, 117, 124, 127, 150, 152
Grossinger, Marguerite Tregre, 18, 20, 21, 28, 59–75, 78–82, 88, 91, 99, 100, 110, 115, 116, 120, 127, 150, 155
Guillory, Joseph Gregoire, 3, 4
Guillory, Margarita, 3, 4

Haitian Revolution, 13, 85
Hall, Gwendolyn Midlo, 2
Hanmer, Aline Dupuy, 90, 93, 107
Hanmer, Erwin, 93
Haydel, Christophe, 22
Haydel, Seraphine, 22–26
Heno, Almaide Dupuy, 84–90, 98, 100, 141, 142, 147
Heno, Eugene Louis, 146, 147
Heno, George, 88, 146, 157
Heno, Jean Baptiste, 88
Heno, Paul, 83, 88, 90, 93, 95, 96, 98, 110, 147
Heno, Pierre, 146
Hobbs, Allyson, 20, 155
Hoggatt, Emma, 43, 89
Hungary, 76, 77, 91

Immaculate Conception Catholic Church, 83, 84, 91, 142

Jim Crow laws, 9, 18, 81, 107, 119, 121, 139
Jourdain, Jean Baptiste, 153

King, Grace, 100, 107, 108
Kinsley, Rufus, 65, 66

Lafourche Parish, LA, 31, 34, 38, 40
Lanauze, Adolphe, 133
Lanauze, P. Henry, 123, 125, 132–49, 154
Lanusse, Armand, 106
Latrobe, John, 101–3
Leathers, Thomas P., 49, 50, 54, 55
LeBourgeois, Joseph, 7

Lind, Jenny, 37, 41, 43
Locoul, Elisabeth, 79
Locoul, Raymond, 67
Lombard, Leonard, 84
Louisiana Native Guard, 25–28, 68–71, 79, 157
Louisiana Purchase, 14, 19, 85, 89, 101
Louisiana Supreme Court, xi, 35, 39, 40, 130, 146
Loving v. Virginia, 151
Luzenberg, Chandler C., 135, 138

Magnolia steamboat, 36, 37, 40–43, 61
manumission, 4, 14, 17, 22, 39, 40
Mary, Aristide, 153
Messner, Juanita, 94
Miller, Lavinia, 76
Milon, Henriette, 131, 132
miscegenation, 54, 81, 124, 126, 127, 130, 134, 135, 148, 151, 155
Mitaud, Josephine, 147

Native Americans, 5, 10, 11
Natchez steamboat, 29, 30, 42, 47, 49–51, 54, 55
New Orleans, LA, xii, 1, 4, 8, 11, 14–19, 21, 22, 24–27, 30, 31, 35, 38, 40–58, 60, 65, 67, 68, 70–72, 75–78, 80, 85–90, 92–97, 101, 105–10, 119, 122–25, 127–36, 139–41, 144, 146–54

Ohio, 38–40, 44
Oliver, Joseph "King," 7
Ory, Edward "Kid," 7

passing, racial, 18–21, 56, 57, 94, 118–25, 128, 134, 141, 155
Perret, P. C., 136
Pinchback, P. B. S., 20, 39
plaçage, 102–6
Plaquemines Parish, LA, 130

Plessy v. Ferguson, 20, 119–22, 154
Potter, Eliza, 76, 106
Prados family, 142, 143
Pratt, George King, 115, 116

"race flagging," 148, 154
rape, 64–67
Reconstruction, 39, 54–57, 81, 95, 98. 108, 118, 134, 143, 153
Rivarde Achille, Sr., 24, 26
Rivarde Achille, II, 80
Rivarde, Achille, III, 79, 80
Robin, C. C., 101
runaway slaves, 11, 34, 67, 68, 88

Sauvinet, Charles, 153
Schaeffer, William, 34
segregation, 18, 81, 119–21, 126, 139, 150, 154
Separate Car Act, 119, 154
Ship Island, 69, 70, 72, 152
Sisters of the Holy Family, 105, 106, 109, 133
St. Augustine Catholic Church, 110
St. Domingue, 13, 84, 100, 109, 140–42
St. James Parish, LA, 27, 41, 62, 69, 81, 108, 157
St. John the Baptist Parish, LA, 2, 4, 7, 22, 23, 26–28, 68, 69, 91
St. Joseph Catholic Church, 48, 53, 54, 59, 78, 81, 116, 117, 124
St. Louis Cathedral, 23, 24, 84, 100, 109, 140–42
St. Louis Cemetery No. 1, 74, 153
St. Louis Cemetery No. 2, 58
Stuard, Armantine Perret, 61–64, 66–68, 80, 116
Stuard, Justin, 80

Thibodaux, Henry Claiborne, 32, 33
Thibodaux, LA, 31, 32
Thomasson, Alexander, 31–36, 38–43, 51, 52, 116
Thomasson, Alfred, 39, 44, 46
Thomasson, Emma, 39, 43, 44, 46, 53
Thomasson, Eugenie, 33
Thomasson, Ferriol, 32, 33
Thomasson, Milly, 33–35, 37–40, 43, 44, 46, 51, 118
Thomasson, St. Clair, 32, 33, 36, 37, 43
Thompson, Doris, 154
Tonnelier, Marguerite, 146
Treadway, Josephine Lightell, 129, 130, 132, 138
Treadway, Octave, 129, 130, 132, 138
Tregre, Séverin, 62, 63
Tremé, 24, 25, 86, 90, 106, 119

Union Army, 7, 27, 49, 68, 71, 72, 77, 80, 91
United States Supreme Court, 18, 35, 121, 151

Vacherie, LA, 27, 157
van Alstyne, Lawrence, 66
Vickery, Veronica, 125, 139
Vital Records Department (New Orleans), 144–46, 154
von Buelow, Edward, 128–30, 150
von Buelow, Ezilda Duvigneaud, 128–30, 150

Warmoth, Henry Clay, 153
White League, 133, 134
Wilkerson, Isabel, 8, 9
Williamson, Joel, 18, 121
Wiltz, Marie Félicité, 133